RUNNING FROM FEAR

Walking Into the Desert and Finding Life Again

THAD CUMMINGS

RUNNING FROM FEAR: *Walking Into the Desert and Finding Life Again*

ISBN: 978-0-9993850-0-5 (Paperback)
ISBN: 978-0-9993850-1-2 (E-book)

Library of Congress Control Number: 2017915190

Cover Photo Credit: Brad Reed, www.ToddandBradReed.com

Printed in the United States of America

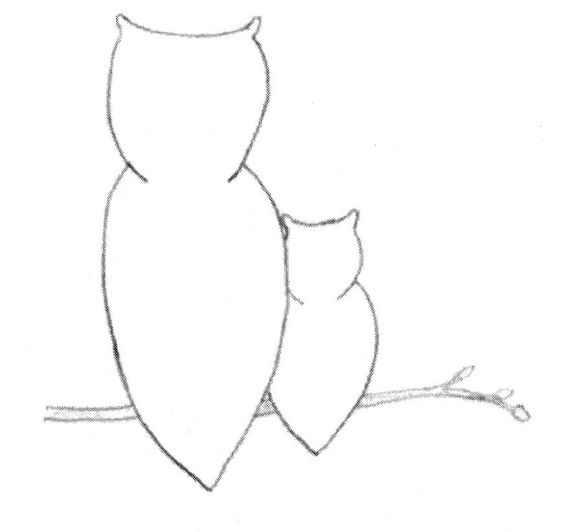

Table of Contents

Acknowledgements

This book is only possible because of the countless people, mentors, teachers, authors, therapists, spiritual directors, friends and strangers who have shared their stories and wisdom with me over the years. It is because of their guidance that I was able to enter and face my own story to be able to share this with you today. This book is meant to be a gift that came from the interconnectedness of hundreds of people, not just me.

A special thanks to the many who have listened to me rant, critiqued and edited these pages to help sort out the mess in my head and get it organized on paper. And to people like Marcia who set aside their own workload to spend dozens of hours making sure my book actually looks like a book.

All the credit does not fall to me because my name is on the cover. We truthfully do nothing or create anything in this life alone, that is the beauty of it.

Introduction

It is one of my most vivid memories going back to that perfectly crisp Michigan fall day in 2011. I was working out with my sister-in-law at the gym. She was tirelessly trying to lose weight after giving birth to her second child and asked if I could help. We were ending the night by jogging a mile and she was pushing herself as fast as she could so I decided to follow suit. I was three minutes into a full blown sprint when my heart started pacing around 180 beats per minute. Getting light headed I decided to hop off the treadmill and bring my heart rate back under control as I was uncomfortably queasy. I stepped outside to let the cool air dance off the beads of sweat coming down my cheeks, hoping for a sigh of relief. A few minutes went by, then five, then ten minutes and my heart was still pacing in the 150s; this had never happened before. My sister-in-law could see how pale I was and asked if we should head out, to which I eagerly agreed.

I drove her home and decided to head for my folks' house just down the road. On a normal day it would not be uncommon for my resting heart rate to hover around 55 beats per minute, but after twenty minutes not only had my heart continued to race, my hands and feet began to tingle. The three-mile drive began to feel like a cross country road trip. I called my parents to let them know I was getting nervous driving so they met me at the end of their long, steep driveway. After putting the car in park I stood up out of the car, but my legs were so weak that I hardly made it three or four steps before they gave way. I sat there on the cold, damp driveway taking long, slow, deep breaths as my heart continued to flutter in my chest. The tingling in my hands and feet had turned into a painful, numbing sensation like when you wake up in the middle of the night after your arms fall asleep. It was slowly spreading from my hands to my forearms to my elbows up towards my shoulders. I could not sit up anymore and had to lay down. I still distinctly remember the pleasant aroma of decaying fall leaves; it was as if all of my senses were in overdrive.

My muscles began contracting in the most unpleasant ways and I found myself seized up in the fetal position. By this point my stepfather had called an ambulance while I began to feel my stomach tighten, followed by my chest. I could not comprehend what was going on with my body but now I began to accept my fate. I started thinking to myself, "This must be it," as every single muscle in my body was in an intense, contorted, excruciatingly painful spasm. It was like getting a foot or a calf cramp and the stabbing pain that comes with it that leaves you rolling around on the floor. That cramp just happened to be covering my entire body. Yet there was no impulse to scream, I was just uttering over and over again, "I'm sorry, tell her I love her, I'm sorry, I'm sorry, I'm sorr, I sor..." Words came to an end as my airway tightened to a close and I could no longer speak. I was paralyzed within my own body but my mind was still racing. My lips felt swollen like balloons and my tongue was like a lead weight I could hardly move. I can still taste the dirt and feel the gravel on my mother's hand pulling my tongue out of my throat, trying to help me breathe as she screamed at my stepfather to tell them to hurry.

What happens next is a bit bizarre and uncomfortable to say, but the only thing I can relate it to is a peaceful bliss. Once you accept the thought that this is the end and you are about to pass away, nothing else really matters. I wasn't begging for more time, I wasn't thinking about bills, or my business, or graduating school, or what I had to do tomorrow. I wasn't holding any resentments or grudges or ill wills towards anybody. All I wanted to do was ask for forgiveness and leave a message of love. It was that simple. By the time I had made it to the hospital and they had doped me up with enough Ativan to knock out a small horse, I was coming back to reality and coming to terms with what my first panic attack looked like. Quite frankly, I was also coming to terms with how much pain I was going to be in for several days. It felt like I had just done two hours of hot yoga, six rounds of kickboxing and dead lifted three times my body weight. I crammed this all into one of Thad's-Butt-Buster-Workout-Sessions (copyright pending). Everything hurt.

Now you'd think afterwards I would be grateful to be alive singing "A Whole New World" to strangers on the street, but after enough conversations with doctors and enough Googling, hearing the repeated phrase, "Well that isn't normal," terrified me. It left one thing plaguing my thoughts — not *if*, but *when* will it happen again.

This moment was certainly dramatic for me, but we all have moments of intense fear that help shape our lives. Fear has been a tool that has helped us survive through the ages. At some point I'm sure you've heard of our basic mammalian instincts, our fight or flight response. It's the response that makes you freeze when you see a bear, when a mother protects her child from any threat, when we escape from a violent situation. But the fear I'm interested in talking about is not just the big fears of life but the subtle fears that control our everyday lives. The fear that drives us to work at jobs we don't really like, to have road rage when someone forgot their blinker, that drives us to drink and to binge watch Netflix. The fear that keeps us from being honest, makes us isolate and hide our true selves from the world and our own families. It is my personal belief and experience that fear in and of itself is the sole driver of pain, grief, isolation, and detachment from our loved ones, communities, and the world. It is what builds the barriers, segregates and destroys. Fear is what ultimately robs us of joy and our ability to thrive in an already difficult and trying world. The fear I want to discuss ranges from faint and nagging to the fear that can leave us paralyzed, literally or metaphorically.

This book is about my journey through my proverbial hell and back, stories about how I've come to understand fear, and the steps I've taken to find a new state of being for myself. Chances are if you are reading this, you may be looking for a step forward as well. We don't typically volunteer to go into the hard places or face our fears for fun; most of it comes out of despair and vulnerability, trusting that better things are yet to come.

There are many folks who dedicate their lives to researching topics like fear and how they affect our lives. While science and experience can go hand in hand, the primary focus of this book is not to get lost in the scientific data. Experts on the matter like Dr. Brené Brown, Dr. Tali Sharot, and Dr. Alex Korb are great resources for the science behind the matter. Personally, I hold no PhD, I am not a psychologist nor do I study neurosciences. I'm simply one man who's been lucky enough to walk through my own desert and face my own fears while simultaneously being graced by the compassion of countless others. Others who have shared the stories of their struggles, their journeys and their wisdom along the way. I'm learning with you, not coming from a place where I have it all figured out and I must tell you. I come to you with a broken past, broken stories and many, many mistakes. I have tasted pain more than I care to remember and I have spread that pain to those closest to me more than I want to admit.

In the end, it is not about justifying fears or trying to dismiss them. Our pain matters. There is not one single person who has not been touched by sorrow and affected by fear in one form or another. This is about acknowledging common struggles we all share, and overcoming the power they have to separate us and seeing the power they have to unite us. At its core, this book is about taking steps towards facing our fears so they no longer control our lives.

I hope you find some things that challenge you, some things that you agree with as well as some things that you do not. Perhaps something that stirs a feeling deep in your soul, even if it makes you uncomfortable, allowing you to realize you aren't crazy or alone. Ultimately, I hope you find the strength to take a step forward, a step towards answering a question on this difficult, chaotic, beautiful, rollercoaster ride we call life.

The following chapters stem from six questions I've dissected over the years: What is fear? How are we afraid? Where does fear come from? How do we face that fear? How do we overcome that fear? And how do we live with that fear? If you find it helpful, each chapter has a section to reflect on some thoughts with guided questions.

Let's journey together.

PART 1

UNCOVERING THE FEAR

If you let the mistakes of your past define the present, you will never have a future.

1

FEAR AS THE ROOT OF ALL EVIL:

how I've come to understand and define fear

> Fear: (noun) an unpleasant emotion caused by the belief that someone or something is dangerous, likely to cause pain, or a threat (Merriam-Webster Dictionary, 2017).

There can be a fine line between healthy behavior and being emotionally or physically controlled by fear. On one side, anxiety and panic are the extreme examples of fear when it consumes us in very blunt ways. On the other side, fear can be helpful and motivating in our everyday lives, especially when we have a strong conceptual understanding of consequences. When the alarm goes off at 6 am and you have to drag yourself into the shower for another day's work, perhaps the fear of getting fired for not showing up keeps you going. It's why most people tend to hit their brakes when they see a cop hiding on the side of the road, whether they were speeding or not. It can be why some of us easily go to the doctor and some of us avoid going to the doctor at all costs. It can be why our palms get sweaty on first dates and why our stomachs drop when that particular person calls. Whether it is seen as a positive or a negative, fear plays a role in almost every one of our decisions. But I think it has more control on our everyday lives than we may be willing to admit, especially when our simple fears distort and become subtle or direct anxieties.

> Anxiety: (noun) a feeling of worry, nervousness, or unease, typically about an imminent event or something with an uncertain outcome (Merriam-Webster Dictionary, 2017).

This definition of anxiety may feel more applicable to our lives. Particularly that part at the end about uncertain outcomes. What really is 100% for certain in this life besides the cheesy answer of death and taxes? Whether it is just semantics, I will leave up to you, but I do want to point out that while there is not a huge difference in the definitions between fear and anxiety, the varying effects can be enormous. Anxiety is often seen as people pale-faced standing in front of a crowd or shaking on an airplane waiting for takeoff. But anxiety can be subtle when it unconsciously affects your actions throughout the day; you begin to make decisions based on it without even knowing it. When I was diagnosed with generalized anxiety disorder and later panic disorder, I thought I was unique (not in the good way). But the more I've engaged with people, the more I've come to realize there isn't a single person I've ever met that doesn't have anxiety affect them in some way, shape or form. It begs the question, what are we really afraid of?

Without making it dramatic or extreme, think of anything you might do in your life or even something you have to do today and try to determine if fear somehow plays a role in it. Don't judge it, condemn it, or dismiss it; simply examine it and discern if fear plays any part in this situation. Take a minute and see if you come up with anything.

Starting out very simply, what is it about climbing ladders, or seeing a rat, or boarding a plane, or getting your teeth cleaned that causes your heart rate to increase? Why do we scream at snakes, put locks on our doors, get anxious speaking in front of audiences, avoid certain areas; why do some people own guns or carry mace? These are easy and obvious fears and we can be pretty quick to say that many people are afraid of a plane crash, or falling off a roof, or having their home broken into. I'd call these surface level fears because most of them are so common and simultaneously so easy to talk about. There is no shame in admitting that you are afraid of getting bitten by a snake, even if it is just a harmless garter snake.

However, what about fears that aren't so obvious? Why do we nearly kill ourselves, sacrifice our free time, life experiences and joy to save for retirement on the hopes of one day that may never come? Why do we tell our kids they essentially have to get college degrees when a job may not be waiting for them, or they may end up doing something they hate out of obligation to societal norms? Why do churches fight over the meaning of a text claiming ultimate superiority in knowledge of the word of God? What leads us to ever justify the need to scream at our spouses when we know it ultimately won't do one bit of good?

I'm not going to argue that putting some money aside and being financially responsible is a bad thing, but with a shrinking middle class, retirement is out of the question for many Americans. College degrees certainly help advance younger generations forward with knowledge and responsibility, but according to the Organization for Economic Co-operation and Development (OECD), the United States ranks 27th in math and science out of the top 34 countries in the world. We can most certainly learn value in differences of opinions, but growing up in Christian communities I've found it more common than not for people to judge, hate and disregard others based on their interpretations of the same book and what they claim to be truth.

If the United States is number one in the world, then depending on which study you look at, why do we rank 14th or 15th on the Global Happiness Index? Even if you would disregard a study like the happiness index, there are a lot of factors that point to this very question. Author and psychologist Brene Brown puts it very plainly when she says, "We are the most in-debt, obese, addicted and medicated adult cohort in U.S. history."

The most influential question I have had circling my thoughts for as long as I've been attempting to save the world was, why? Why are we so depressed, so angry, so money and success hungry, so addicted to reality TV, to sports, to social media or to working? Why do we have such high divorce rates? Why is it easier to play with our smartphones than play with our kids? Why is it so much easier to avoid talking to our neighbor than having any form of meaningful community relationship? Why do we get together and only have small talk about the weather and avoid any potential truth that our lives may be, well, less than perfect or that we don't have all of our poop in a group? Why is the world in such peril, the environment being destroyed, and people struggling everywhere?

My work began with trying to solve one issue at a time until I realized I wasn't solving anything, nor ultimately helping anyone, but simply trying to patch the Titanic with SpongeBob Band-Aids. This is the only instance in my life and my search for wisdom where the deeper I dug, the simpler the answer became, not more complicated. Fear, for me, from my experience in life, from what I've seen, witnessed, and heard from countless others, is the driving force behind the pain and brokenness in this world.

Fear, in and of itself, is the root of all evil.

Understanding why fear is the root of all evil is not as simple as giving ten more examples and calling it a day. This entire book is dedicated to not only understanding this concept, but how to address it. To make a sweeping statement like this and understand it in its entirety means digging deep and facing things we don't normally face.

I firmly believe all fear stems from two concise trains of thought; the fear of not being enough and the fear of not being in control. But fear is like an onion, we have to peel back layer after layer to get to the thing behind the thing that is really, behind the thing. So before we dive into facing our fears, how to handle them, and how to take a step forward with them, we have to first look at how we avoid them.

CHAPTER 1 NOTES AND REFLECTIONS

Start out easy and list your fears. What fears control you, keep you from living your life to the fullest? What subtle fears may play a role in your decisions?

2

JUSTIFYING AND AVOIDING FEAR:

starting at square one

We all hold PhDs in how to avoid our fears, but if we don't understand how we avoid them it makes it really difficult to face them. One of the simplest ways to avoid facing our fears is to justify them, which makes for a very easy argument. How many people do you know that secretly can't stand their job, counting the minutes until Friday and praying Monday is a lifetime away? But when you have bills to pay or people that depend on you, it's very easy to justify staying in one place no matter how much discontent it may cause you. When I worked at an inpatient oncology floor with mostly terminal cancer patients, I can't tell you how many dying people in their 30s, 40s, 50s, all the way up to their 90s, stated over and over again, "Life is short, live while you have the chance." But most of us do have the chance and we don't take it or we convince ourselves we can't. I'm not trying to tell a single mother of three, working two jobs, that she needs to give it all up and go and travel Europe. Living life can come in all sorts of different ways, but fear justification can be something that ruins lives. Especially when we use it on ourselves to say we are not good enough, we don't deserve it, or we will never get it so why bother. A very simple question I can ask myself when I go to bed each night is did I start my day with fear over what was to come, what I had to do, how I would pay the bills and what tomorrow would look like, or did I start my day with gratitude, laughing and playing with my daughter? The answer is usually hard for me to swallow because more often than not, fear, not gratitude, starts my day. How can I ultimately justify that? This isn't about denying the very real issues and burdens of life, but changing the viewpoint of how we engage them for our own sanity, because when our justifications run out, avoidance comes into play.

Two of the ways we tend to show fear avoidance is through escaping our fears and through projecting our fears onto others. How we escape is always tailored to our individual personalities shaped by our childhoods and life experiences, but one thing I can promise you for certain is that you escape. Some people point the finger at easy targets like drug-addicts, alcoholics, and the homeless to say they are the root cause of societal issues, they have the problems, and they are the escapists. My goal is to expand that outlook to the rest of us since we are all running from something. And I want to shed light on our tendency to fall back on one common phrase and thought process that ultimately keeps us all stuck:

"I'm not as bad as that person" syndrome.

While I have no intention of debating that binge watching Netflix is safer for our communities than, say, drinking and driving, I am going to argue that you escape regardless and it impacts your life. If you are human, there is a good chance you have a combination of many of the habits listed below and many that I haven't listed. Some of us escape through eating too much, for others it is exercise or starving ourselves on diets, some of us work too much, avoid work entirely, talk at people, or avoid people. It can include getting lost in Facebook, Snapchat, Instagram, reading books, video games and technology, music and art, gambling, hoarding, minimalism, sex, shopping and spending money, volunteering and giving money away, watching sports, playing sports, fishing, farming, being outdoors, activism, boycotting or politics. We may be enablers, we may have intense denial, some build walls, we fight, we are stubborn, others are passive, or submissive, letting people walk all over us and we hide. The list can be never ending. Now at this point something should have given you pause to say, "Ok, I get how drugs or spending eight hours a day staring at my cell phone may be an escape, but how are things like art or volunteering or standing up for a cause a form of escape?" The answer is, easily. You see, having a drink isn't necessarily a bad thing, watching a movie isn't necessarily a bad thing, educating someone on a healthier diet or a just cause are never necessarily bad things. It's when these things consume us and we lose all concept of reality that we become addicts to whatever that escape is.

At my peak, I owned multiple social, ethical and save-the-world companies. I had donation programs, worked with many non-profits, started my own non-profit and fed hundreds of people free meals every week. I'd spend every waking hour trying to figure out how to improve the world, from reducing slave labor in our cheap manufactured goods, to fighting environmental pollution, to helping those in need. The more I learned about the issues of the world, the more I thought it was up to me to solve them. Fear drove me to the brink of death, literally, and I believed that I was never going to be enough unless I saved the world. An impossible task, which even I knew to be true. People applauded me and cheered me on everywhere I went as I worked non-stop 7 days a week without taking a vacation in almost a decade. Everyone except those closest to me, who felt my burden the most and saw what it was doing to our relationships and to me.

My escape into saving the world, volunteering, and activism became toxic when I believed the world would be a better place if everyone thought, acted, believed and did as I did. All I needed to do was show everyone how. Truthfully, all I really did was isolate myself from those around me as I constantly projected onto them that they were also not enough if they didn't compost, recycle, buy organic, bike to work, eat healthy, own less stuff, volunteer, buy ethical products, etc. The list was so long that even I couldn't keep up with it. Now again, things like buying non-slave-labor clothes and food are never bad things; most would agree it's a wonderful thing we should all be doing. But when your values and opinions come at the expense of your personal relationships and most people can't stand to be around you, well, what was I really accomplishing short of alienating myself from the world? I dwindled my close relationships down to those who thought just like me and I pushed the rest aside.

At our core, we all want to be heard and we all want to be loved, but it has to start with knowing *we are enough*. Until we know that we are enough, we cannot adequately care about anything else long term without a high likelihood of failure. And man, when I failed, did I fail hard. More on that to come.

I want to wrap up fear avoidance and "I'm not as bad as that person" syndrome as bluntly as I can. There will always be somebody who is "worse," just like there is always someone smarter, healthier, richer, poorer, angrier, skinnier, fatter, taller, prettier, stronger and weaker. If I can make one statement jump out of this chapter, it is this: the more you point the finger elsewhere and think that they have it better, or they are the problem, or that country or that culture or that religion or that group, the more you give someone else control over your life. You are avoiding your own fears by projecting them onto someone or something else. This inevitably leaves you helpless to face your own realities.

Whether you are evading the issue by saying, "I'm not as bad as that person so I don't need to change, they do," or you are drowning in self-doubt saying, "Everyone else around me is so much better," or likely a combination of the two, you will stay stuck. You will keep yourself in a place from which you'll be unable to expand, grow and learn on your journey towards greater fulfillment and joy. You have no control over anyone else and what they do. Not in the slightest. I can also promise that you judging them, condemning them, or guilt and shaming them also will not make them want to change.

So what does it truly matter if they are better or worse, based on your opinion of what they should or should not be doing? Climb down from that pedestal and breathe. This is about you, your fears, and your journey because if you really care about others, you can only engage others when you are able to fully engage yourself. However, being able to fully engage yourself means you have to know what your driving force is to say these things or take that specific action in the first place when it comes to avoiding and justifying fears. Sometimes it's easier to understand what we are doing today, if we look back and know where we came from.

CHAPTER 2 NOTES AND REFLECTIONS

In what ways do you escape and avoid fears? In what ways do you justify your actions and fears? Do you use "I'm not as bad as that person" to avoid or justify things you say or do?

3

LOOKING BACKWARDS:

we must face our past in order to make peace with it

Sometimes taking a step forward starts with taking several steps backwards. We all have driving forces in our lives and it is important to understand them. For myself, I needed to understand: Why did I want to really save the world and what was I running from? Peeling back this onion layer is usually the most uncomfortable to face. It often requires looking at things we really don't want to see, things that are better off left alone, left in the past, left unsaid. But, similar to how fear avoidance allows the fear to control us, avoiding our past allows our past to define our future. More often than not, it can define our future in ways we never even notice until it's too late.

My first cognizant memory as a child was around the age of three. I was sitting on the stand in the courtroom screaming and crying for my mother as the judge asked if I would rather live with my mother or my father. It didn't take long to understand that divorce never enters any family without leaving deep pain and scars. I cannot imagine the stress my family and parents were going through at the time, but I can now comprehend the affect it was having on me, even at an early age. Both of my parents were alcoholics, which complicated things immensely. My mother remarried when I was around the age of five and I became the youngest of seven boys. Later, my father remarried for a third time and added a whole other dimension of complications to the family. I split time, living mostly with my mother in Michigan and visiting my father in North Carolina. To say the least, it was a colorful childhood.

For the first two decades of my life I would get a taste of many forms of abuse from psychological and emotional abuse, to physical, verbal and neglectful abuse. I would get to see what alcohol, drugs and violence can do to people. I learned how easily families and friends could be torn apart over and over again. I would see people beat, cheat and steal from their own, knowing there was nothing I could do. I saw how fear, grief, pain and despair could bring out the worst in people. I lost track of how many funerals I went to, from kids my own age to grandparents. I watched people with tumors the size of grapefruits wither away to nothing, and I gazed deeply into my father's eyes the moment before he went into a coma. Pain and death was all around me and it was a game for my siblings to convince me that everything was going to kill me. I became terrified of everything and losing everyone. Yet, the most damaging thing for me, was having the thought that I was never going to be enough, or ever amount to anything, physically and verbally engrained into me.

To make matters more convoluted, at a very early age I was convinced that I needed to turn to God for the answers. Young minds are dangerously malleable, especially when it comes to grandiose stories. When the adults around you can't help you out, nor can your siblings, family members or friends, it only makes sense to a child that a higher power must exist. But when I entered that realm of religion, I was given a very particular story over and over again; I was not enough, I was a sinner, and I deserved what I received. If the stories from those who influenced me most in my childhood were also supported by the ultimate divine entity in the cosmos, then it must all be true. I am not enough, it was my fault, and the task to salvation is as impossible as life itself. This became my "wounded child," something we all have. It's the place within my soul where I stored the pain and grief that I could not understand or comprehend, and it left a fiery inferno of rage burning deep inside me. Nothing could touch it.

When my father died during my senior year of high school, my religion died with him. Not the bad parts from my childhood; if I could only be so lucky. No, I lost what remaining hope I had left. I began to retreat from the world, shutting down to friends, getting drunk and crying myself to sleep every night. Suddenly out of the blue, like a cheesy Hallmark movie, a gift came back with this sorrow stronger than ever. I could see pain. I mean really see pain, and in everyone. Now, I could see this pain for as long as I could remember; I could see people unhappy and always wanted to help, even as a child. But now I could walk into a room and just feel it: it was in her posture, it was in his gaze, the way they breathed, the way that person tried to convince me how happy they were, and all I could do was sigh. Most days I thought that I was crazy, but the minute I stopped running around trying to pretend everything was ok, countless people began sharing their pain with me. Not because I was anything special, not because I had anything figured out, but because I started looking people in the eyes and asking how they were really doing. The stories of anguish, grief, remorse and anxiety were at times more than I could grasp.

I met people with stories that felt much harder than mine, that I could not comprehend, and I met people with stories that didn't seem so bad. I've sat with people who lost a pet, who lost their spouse, who lost their child, who lost children. I've sat with people whose bodies were covered with scars from cutting themselves, people who starved themselves and those who nearly ate themselves to death. People afraid to look in the mirror and people who could not stop looking in the mirror. People who had made millions and lost it, people who didn't know how to pay their next bill. People addicted to cigarettes, people addicted to booze and people addicted to heroin. People whose family members had raped them, people who struggled with porn. People who wanted to end their life and people who were afraid their life was about to be taken. People dying at 90 and people dying at 20. People who felt they were the victims and people who felt they were to blame. Most commonly, people who struggled with shame, guilt and resentment. How people responded and carried these burdens with them was always unique, but the pain was universal in everyone I met. You see, when looking at our own stories it's very easy to get lost in comparing oneself to another and saying, "I did not have it as bad," or "they did not have it as bad as me so how can they ________?"

It's important never to play this game. It's another version of the game that will only keep us stuck and prevent us from moving on with our own journey, let alone truly seeing someone else in their sorrows. This pain can either divide us or unite us because we all have broken parts of our story. Some things may be more obvious than others, but I have never met anyone who was not affected by the brokenness of their childhood or life, who was not molded by it in some way, shape or form. To say that you weren't molded, would be to say that you are perfect, and I haven't met anyone perfect yet!

A light bulb went on. I stopped drinking, I stopped hiding and I made a decision that I was going to prove my family wrong, I was going to prove my childhood wrong, and I was going to show God how worthy I really was and prove Him wrong. I was going to find my worth out there, I was going to be someone, I was going to become <u>enough</u>.

It was time to save the world ... or so I thought.

CHAPTER 3 NOTES AND REFLECTIONS

What are some of the things from your past that shaped you? What incidents or experiences may have caused you to have fear? To withdraw? To act out?

4

DON'T TAKE ~~EVERYTHING~~ ANYTHING PERSONALLY:

the journey to looking at others through new eyes, begins first by looking at yourself

The tricky thing about engaging the world is if you don't begin with a solid foundation, it's amazing how little it takes to throw your whole day off. How many times in your life have you been driving in traffic and ended up either flipping someone the bird, or receiving the bird yourself? Maybe you've even been the recipient of a long, drawn out horn blaring session with perhaps some choice words we don't need to mention. The other day I was driving on the highway following all legal road laws when someone made four traffic violations to swerve around me and hold their finger out the window for an unnecessary amount of time. I ended up having to pass this gentleman several miles later, which always makes for an awkward road moment. If I were to be honest, for most of my driving years I would have used this passing moment to yell, or honk, or return the gestured finger. That is until I understood the second agreement in Don Miguel Ruiz's book, *The Four Agreements*. The second agreement is, "Don't take anything personally." I've come to understand it as, "the thing behind the thing." Or as I heard the author and speaker Rob Bell say it once, "the thing, behind the thing, that's really behind the thing."

Now I want to make it very clear that I did not read Mr. Ruiz's book and magically feel enlightened, smiling at every car that cut me off while wishing them the best. Actually, I chucked the book across the room after reading that chapter, calling it hogwash; I took another nine months to finish the remaining 70 pages and another four years to actually understand it. If someone comes up to you and tells you that you are a terrible employee, you're a lousy friend, engages in physical or verbal abuse, or is simply that guy cutting me off in traffic, how can we not take it personally? What would I say to my wounded child every morning waking up in panic from a night terror, "Don't take it personally, Thad"? Of course not, nothing is that simple. But like everything else we will discuss in this book, not taking it personally is ultimately about regaining control of our joy and not letting someone else rob us of it.

I don't know the story of that man from the highway, I don't know what pain or grief he was suffering from that made him flip me the bird. His wife could have left him, he could have been struggling to pay his bills, maybe he just lost his job or his boss yelled at him. There are a million things that could have been going wrong in his day, but before we look at someone else's story, we need to first understand this concept for ourselves. We have a bigger story driving our everyday stories. Once we have a firm grasp on where our bigger story comes from, we have the capability to make peace with our past and begin adding to our foundation of joy to share that with others. Perhaps there will even be a little less road rage and car accidents in the world.

Let's start at step one here and level the playing field for a minute. This means playing the comparison game is off the table. It is very safe to say that we all do harm, we all say bad things, and we all make mistakes. A commonality that we all share is also a simple truth; we are all incredibly imperfect creatures. If I were giving a speech right now we'd have that awkward small chuckle coming from the crowd, not because it's funny, but because it's true. The minute we get back in tune with that, the more grace and forgiveness we can tap into to begin healing ourselves and our relationships. The journey to finding compassion starts within, since we are usually our own worst critics. Let me make it clear that giving ourselves grace only helps us grow stronger and reduce the number of times we repeat the same mistakes, those ones we seem to repeat over and over again. And I think we can tap into more grace when we stop pointing the finger elsewhere and find humility within. The saying goes, point a finger at someone else and you will have three fingers pointing back at yourself. We heard it so many times as kids that we are almost numb to it. But those three fingers are where I have found the most humility and thus the most revelations. So next let's set aside the world's issues for a moment, the pain from our past, the pain we've passed on, and the finger-pointing, to take a minute and look in the mirror.

Remember how I said I believed the world would be a better place if everyone thought, acted and did as I did? I was one of the foremost environmentalists in my community striving for big changes. I just forgot to mention a few minor details to people along my quest. For example, I drove at least 30,000 miles a year in my car consuming hundreds of gallons of fuel directly funding some of the atrocities of war and genocide in the Middle East. Don't worry, it was a hybrid. But that hybrid was jam packed with batteries that were composed of precious metals like cobalt, likely mined in South Africa where it is common to see even kids mining by hand in some of the worst environmental and inhumane conditions. The batteries are then put together in sometimes just as inhumane working and environmental conditions in China. It also goes for the laptop I'm currently typing on, my smartphone, and just about every electronic gadget I own. There is a human and environmental price tag that comes with my life's luxuries that those in extreme poverty pay for, not me. I enjoy the convenience of cheap electricity whenever I turn on my light switch, and fail to remember that up to 90% of it comes from coal and natural gas power. I'll never forget the first time I saw mountaintop removal coal mines, which have destroyed tens of thousands of acres of precious forests and ecosystems permanently, not to mention decimating local towns with toxic water and high cancer rates. I even ate processed food from time to time which supported large swaths of mono crops and concentrated animal farms.

From American workers to third world countries to the environment to the animals, everyone was paying for the externalized costs to support my quick, convenient and affordable way of life. When I sat with the three fingers pointing back at me, I realized I could destroy my entire environmentalist foundation in all of five minutes. What's worse is I said bad things to good people, I dismantled friendships, and hurt many people close to me including my own partner and child, whom I was everything but present for. All of this was while I was out attempting to "save the world."

I have a list of baggage just as long as the list of baggage I tried to project out onto the world, and that was hard to come to terms with. I would judge people just by their grocery carts for not forking up an extra 25 cents to get organic bananas when they were buying soda. I judged everyone, constantly. Why? Because I could not stop judging myself. This was where it came full circle. I earnestly believed I would never be enough until I saved the world. I was smart enough to understand that was an impossible task. However, if my goal was to save the world, I could not take breaks, I did not deserve a vacation, there was always, always more work to be done, and more projects to start. One company wasn't enough, I needed three, three wasn't enough, how can I create copy-and-paste models? A community garden wasn't even going to feed a neighborhood, how would I develop large scale, self-sustaining agriculture systems? Ok, this model could work, but what about different climates; we are talking about feeding thousands of people, but there are billions in the world. What about famine in Africa, the drought in the Middle East, what about war and poverty and genocide and pollution and environmental destruction and loss of resources?

I was drowning.

I began to comprehend what I was doing, why I was doing it and how terrible it was for me. I was building up the knowledge and tools, but I could not stop. Do you know the feeling? It is easy to become quickly lost in the enormity of the world's problems, or work problems or family, spouse and kid problems, or even just life problems, and have a meltdown. But sometimes a meltdown is exactly what we need. Sometimes a meltdown can turn knowledge into wisdom. Wisdom then allows us to confront our underlying fears and take one more step forward.

I truly believe meltdowns can be where most people find their "things behind the thing." I found personally and from others that the most change and personal growth occurs from seasons of hardship or when we are forced to change. It's very rare that we wake up one day and say, "My life is going so perfectly I'm going to quit my job and give up eating pizza just for fun." It's more common that we change when the doctor calls, when we lose our job, a spouse leaves or a loved one passes and change is staring us square in the face. Personally, I've been lucky enough to have two meltdowns in my life thus far. I put emphasis on lucky because I completely missed the ball on the first one. I tell you this not to drag out a few more pages, but to reluctantly show that this journey forward from fear is not a straight arrow for any of us. It looks a bit more like a friend trying to walk a straight line after half-off-martini-night downtown. A lot of zigzagging, some backwards steps, a few falls with bumps and bruises, and in extreme cases, dinner ending up all over that new sport coat. It's hard, it's painful and it can even be embarrassing, but with enough determination, you will make it through that crosswalk even if it takes several friends helping you out along the way.

The first meltdown came when my daughter was born. I had been terribly sick for almost two years and was losing the ability to hide it. What started out as a simple stomach issue had turned into vomiting every morning when I woke up. Back pain turned into an inability to put on my shoes some mornings. Infections ravaged my body, parasites plagued me, organs began to fail, I was losing weight no matter how much I ate, and my skin was beginning to turn that goldenrod yellow from jaundice. You could play the xylophone on my rib cage and my brother gave me the nickname "skeletor." My heart was lucky to beat consistently for more than twenty minutes at a time and threw me into a panic every time it started skipping beats. I reluctantly waited each day, expecting it to simply stop during one of those episodes. No matter how many doctors I saw, or pills I took, I kept getting worse. It was painful to eat and I was constantly nauseated. If someone across the street sneezed, I would be sick the next day and I was always, always sick. I didn't have much left of my immune system nor any energy and was in a continuous state of exhaustion. I thought my end was really coming at this point and I didn't have the guts to tell anyone, especially my own pregnant fiancé. Terrified of my demise, I was too afraid to tell anyone so I let people know I wasn't feeling well, and I hid the truth as best as I could for another year. I spent each working moment trying to secure enough to pass on to my new family so my partner and our child could live a comfortable life. I was also beginning to give up on the notion of saving the world, drowning in pity and self-doubt and realizing there are more problems in the world than I will ever be able to touch. I call it the screw it point most environmentalists go through after understanding that the world may be beyond repair. If I was going to perish, what did I really accomplish and how could this be the way to go? Forget not taking anything personally, this was my life I was talking about. After all, if I was trying to save the world, why would fate choose me?

December 4th, 2014 came. Fear took on a whole new meaning when our hospital room went from a nurse to a staff of almost a dozen wearing all different scrub colors. Our daughter was born blue as a Smurf, unwilling to breathe. I was trembling as the seconds felt like hours, mumbling to God that "You cannot take her." I had no knowledge of what was actually happening as I stared at her mother whose blood pressure was through the roof. The intense swelling in her legs had left me in a constant state of panic for a week. I'd been worried that she may have preeclampsia and something might happen to her too after all the issues the baby was having in the womb.

Alas, a breath of air and a faint cry as our child was loaded into what I could only describe as a spaceship for babies to be carted to the neonatal intensive care unit (NICU). As the fears subsided and mom drifted off to sleep, I sat there in the NICU staring into my daughter's eyes. It struck me that my problems were so far beyond my own selfishness. Trying to comprehend conception through pregnancy and to birth, I was literally looking at the miracle of life itself. I don't know how else you could honestly describe it with words that wouldn't somehow cheat the awe of it. In the coming days and weeks this wake up call would encircle my thoughts. It was no longer about my story, my pain, or my health issues and I didn't need to take any of it personally. When we leave the world of taking everything personally, it gives us more space for gratitude. The more we embrace gratitude, the more we can serve others and their needs. We leave our self-centered worlds and our eyes begin to see just how much there is to life.

I wish I could end the book there, but it doesn't and I dropped the ball again. My thoughts slowly evolved from gratitude for a new life and a new family back to my self-centered focus. What if I pass on the pain from my childhood to my partner and daughter? Forget saving the world, am I enough to be a father, am I enough to be a husband? Moreover, I haven't saved the world, so who am I to deserve a family of my own? I became convinced that I was going to fail my new family and so it was back to the drawing board to make them proud, no matter what the cost. After all, this was the world my daughter was going to inherit. I knew that when the time came and she looked up to me and wondered why things were so bad, there is one question I refused to let her ask me, "Dad, why didn't you do anything to try and stop this mess"? And damned be to all if my family ever had to wonder about having a roof over their heads or where their next meal would come from. I hopped back on the rollercoaster ride I had just gotten off for only a brief moment.

More companies, more projects, more money, and now I REALLY needed to save the world for my daughter's sake. This came at an expense of enormous shame and guilt which I brought back into my home life. The consistent theme in all of this was nothing was ever enough, and I was never enough. If only I could control it all, then it may be possible. After a couple more years of books, therapists, classes, sermons, and friends, I conceptually understood more than ever what my "thing behind the thing" was. Heck, I could have likely written a book about it then, but that didn't help me address it. All the knowledge in the world can't actually get you there and knowledge doesn't turn into wisdom without some deep, hard work. I was seeing an alternative doctor, I was on a strict diet and pill regimens and my health was slowly beginning to improve. Yet my self-centered focus meant I was back to disregarding everything and everyone. My ability to not take anything personally was all but lost and I was back to working no less than eighty hours a week. Remember that burning inferno inside my soul? Now I was ready to melt steel.

Thankfully, I didn't know my life was about to come to a screeching halt, but I could not be happier that it did.

CHAPTER 4 NOTES AND REFLECTIONS

What are some of your imperfections? How do you point the finger at others and how do you perhaps point the finger at yourself?

5

LOSING IT ALL, TURNING THE CORNER, AND TAKING ONE STEP FORWARD:

when chaos becomes a gift

If you ever ask someone to tell you a story about losing it all, it's shocking what you might hear. Stories of not only sheer despair, but the resilience people can have to endure such losses. It's another universal part of this life that has the power to connect us. By the summer of 2016, I was worth upwards of a million dollars just shy of turning 26. After eight years of non-stop working seven days a week without a vacation, I could finally say I was debt free and had enough financial security to live for years without a worry. The businesses were doing well, the social missions working, the non-profit was finally taking shape, I had many employees and grand visions. Now we lived in a small $70,000 house, drove a used car, and lived a very simple life, but let's just say overall I was really tasting success as defined by American culture. I was also poised to use these resources to make big changes in the world. But by January of 2017, my partner moved out, the companies were gone along with all of the employees, the non-profit no longer had a stream of income; where I was once the guy that loaned others money, I was now borrowing and that cell phone that never stopped going off day or night was now silent.

Nearly a decade of work and accomplishments evaporated in a matter of months and my partner and my new family along with it. Most nights I lay awake staring at the ceiling for hours on end. I would be crying one minute, then cursing the heavens the next. My mind was enraged, trying to understand what had happened, what was happening, and what in the world I was supposed to do next. Sleep was a blessing if I could get it for a few hours in a row. Then I'd wake up to a quiet bed, in an empty apartment, and the swirling shroud of condemnation would begin all over again. The worst question anybody could ask me was how I was doing. What plausible answer could I give beyond the mind numbing generic response of, "good, good and you?" I didn't want to lie but I also was too ashamed to be honest. I was just never prepared for how quickly the tide could turn and I spent the next six months hiding from everyone.

So how did I get to this point and what really went wrong that summer before life came crashing down? A culmination of dozens of things really, but truthfully it was crashing down long before I realized it. Sometimes when life is moving 100 miles an hour and you are never caught up, you become numbed out to reality. I was in a constant trance-like state. While I was trying to end the world's pain, I became ignorant to the pain right in front of my own eyes; to a daughter who hardly saw her father, to a partner waiting for so much as an "I love you," to my friends that I never spent time with, and even to myself. Joy is not really a word that existed in my vocabulary. The unease in my soul, this nagging itch that was never satisfied, became more and more evident.

I remember sitting in my therapist's office at the beginning of summer when my partner had just asked me to "come home." I was baffled as to what she could mean — I'm home every night! The therapist turned to me and said in the calmest voice, "Oh Thad, do you know that you are enough? Does your wounded child know that he is enough"? Now it wasn't like this was the first person to ask this question or bring it to my attention, but everything in my body was fighting like it never had before. So by time the therapist repeated the original question, "would you ever like to actually come home?", I could not help but lash out. You see, my ego, my pride, that burning inferno inside me was being poked and prodded like taunting a caged beast with a stick. There was no denying my partner and therapist were right, but they were asking me to open the cage to the monster I'd spent my life hiding. A monster of endless fear, fierce anger, frigid loneliness, incessant bitterness and unbounded resentment. This monster was two decades old and comprised of anything I didn't or couldn't face. My response was retaliation. I began pushing everything and everyone away from me as fast and as hard as I could. Anything to keep from confronting that monster. Anything to avoid that pain. Then IT happened; the start of the second meltdown.

It was now the end of summer in 2016 and I was in a very peculiar situation. My friend Kent was the former pastor at my church and that year he took on some work with me at the non-profit. Kent had more wisdom than I could comprehend at times and I was incredibly lucky to get to work with him. This also meant he was able to watch my life come crumbling down during those grievous months. Kent was never fond of giving direct answers, often relating things to parables and asking me questions instead. Most days I could not stand it because we live in a culture that loves answers and so do I. Everyone claims to know them and for just the right price, it can all be yours. This mentality also makes it easy to keep the blame on others when things don't go according to plan. But instead, when someone gives you a question to sit with, it means you have to also sit with your own thoughts and decipher them. It's frustrating, tiring and difficult, but at the end of the day it is incredibly powerful and useful.

Never trust a person, including me, who thinks they have it all figured out and can give you the answers because none of us really know. We may make educated guesses, sure. But the best thing we can do for one another is support each other on our journeys, have grace for one another when we make mistakes, and share the wisdom we've learned along the way. We are all learning in this, together. No one can can tell another what to do because only you know what is ultimately best for you and your wellbeing. Alternatively, we can become a mirror to reflect back different viewpoints and different ways of seeing the uncertainties and struggles we face. The people who have the most influence in our lives don't try to fix our life for us, they simply sit in the pain with us and guide us back to ourselves. They show us that we had the answers within us all along, even if we needed some help finding them.

"When it's all over you'll realize that the answer is already within you." – Andrea Pham

---

I'll never forget the morning we were out weeding in the community garden and Kent turned to me to nonchalantly say, "You know Thad, losing everything that defines you, every label you've come to know, could be the greatest thing that will ever happen to you." When your life feels like a pile of rubble after an earthquake, how do you appropriately respond to that? It is possible I may have mumbled some choice words under my breath. Truthfully though, he could not have been more right, even if I didn't know it at the time.

Kent was in the process of creating a trip called the Wilderness Retreat. A weekend designed to disconnect from the modern world and technology and create an opportunity to engage your inner self. That inner self for me was still that caged beast that everyone kept incessantly poking. Fear is all but consuming when you're looking at this caged beast wondering what would happen if you took the lock off because there is no telling how you will react until you do. It was time to find out and the minute Kent announced the trip, I was the first person who signed up.

Halfway through the weekend I was out in the woods alone doing an exercise where we are encouraged to confront the wounded child from our past. It sounds weird but stay with me, because this is the only way I can describe it in words that may convey the depth of what happened. Have you ever seen the film "Goodwill Hunting"? If not, I hope you can watch it. Towards the end of the movie (spoiler alert), when Robin Williams is saying to Matt Damon over and over again, "It's not your fault Sport, it's not your fault," and Damon breaks down sobbing ... well, that's about the closest explanation I can give you to the conversation I had with my wounded child. I found myself sobbing in the middle of the Wilderness State Park in northern Michigan on a perfectly sunny Saturday morning. Years of anguish were coming out as I helplessly clung to the sticks and leaves. An hour went by, the tears began to dry up, and no joke, a soft golden beam of warm light pierced the forest canopy hitting my face. I sat up to the smell of earth all around me, trying to comprehend what just happened, and my life has never been the same since.

Now this is the part where it would be great if I could say things were peachy from then on. I figured it all out and solved all of life's problems in one fell swoop! In fact, quite the opposite happened. The following Monday my partner and I were sitting back in the therapist's office discussing the separation. I didn't know it was about to happen, but I lost it. The only thing I could say through the waves of tears was, "I don't want to cause any more pain." The beast was loose and it was now chasing my wounded child and there was only enough room inside me for one of them. It would throw everything it had at me to try and knock me off course as I pleaded with God every morning and every night to make it stop. I told my therapist I was ready to take a step forward and it became very clear that before I could make any progress with myself, I'd first have to make peace with my past. That meant facing the demons that lay buried deep in the tomb this beast had been protecting all these years. Every week I sat in her office as she said to me over and over again, "You have the strength to do this, it isn't easy, but you can do this." The next six months would prove to be the most difficult months I've ever faced.

CHAPTER 5 NOTES AND REFLECTIONS

Have you ever "lost it all"? What happened? What are the labels that you would use to define who you are? What would happen if you lost these labels, and are they helpful to begin with? Are they really you?

6

HURT PEOPLE HURT PEOPLE:

my painful moment with the divine

Breakthroughs can come in the most unexpected ways. More often than not, we aren't even ready for them when they come. All those prayers every night and every morning seemed to be a waste of time. If I were being completely honest, I didn't actually believe prayer did any good. It hadn't in my life thus far so what was going to change now? Nor did I actually believe in what some call the "slot machine God" where you say a prayer and wait for it to be magically answered. Kind of like putting a quarter in the machine, pulling that lever and hoping all three cherries line up. Weeks in the therapist's office were turning into months and it was now the spring of 2017. The more time went on, the more my fiery inferno grew. I was not feeling more relieved, I was not feeling less fear, I was feeling more terrified than ever. The guilt, shame and angst were beginning to consume me and I was lucky to sleep three or four hours a night.

There can be many moments in life when we hit bottom. Most people reference it as hitting "rock bottom." Sometimes we need to hit rock bottom and let everything smash to pieces before we can begin putting them back together again in a new way. Here's the thing about rock bottom though; you do not actually know where it is. Every time I thought I was hitting rock bottom, I was not even close. Rock bottom is like taking a deep breath and swimming down to the bottom of a water well to try and grab that golden key of wisdom you dropped. Except you keep swimming and swimming and it's pitch black so you have no idea where the bottom is. Your lungs are compressing, screaming out for a gasp of air while every fiber in your body is twitching, begging, pleading for you to turn back towards the surface. Most of the time, we do. We turn back to the surface without the key. But life will get stormy again and when the clouds get dark enough, we will be forced to try once more.

A friend gave me the book *Sit, Walk, Stand*, by Watchman Nee and there was one reference that stuck with me like glue. When a person is drowning in a lake, in order to save them, you must either wait until they are exhausted and give up, or you must knock them out. If you try and swim to them while they are still fighting, they will drown you with them. I think my therapist was waiting for me to give up on my pride, ego and control over my fear because after those first months I was finally drained. I had no fight left in me and I was ready to drown. She told me to go home that night and ask God to take me into the "hard." Was this her idea of a twisted joke? Am I not already living in hell? How much "harder" can this get? What she meant, I didn't know, but I quietly thought to myself, what harm could it do? After all, prayer hasn't taken me anywhere so far.

That night I knelt down on the floor and simply said out loud, "Alright God, I'm ready, show me what it is I'm missing, take me into the hard." Now I want to preface this by saying my entire life I've dealt with repressed memories one at a time. Through dreams, moments that bring them back, painful triggers; the memories are there, but always one at a time. In this instance, a floodgate opened. I lost complete control over my entire thought process. Repressed memory after memory after memory came rushing into my frontal lobe. It was unlike anything I have ever experienced. Dozens upon dozens of memories surged through my body without any restraint. Memories I hadn't faced since the moment they occurred. Memories I had buried so deep they should have never come back. I could not make them stop, as though they were waves crashing along the shore during a storm, and I found myself curled into a ball weeping uncontrollably. Not at any point had I cried like this before for what felt like hours that may have only lasted minutes. I was screaming at God, cursing God. Unable to withstand any more I pleaded for it to end. Then all of a sudden, just like flicking a light switch, the floodgates closed and it all abruptly ended. I laid there stunned.

What happened next is hard to explain to this day, but I felt no fear. Not the slightest amount about anything. It was the most tranquil moment of peace I'd ever experienced, even more than that day on the driveway when I thought my life was ending. It's how I would imagine a Buddhist reaching Zen must feel. Complete and utter fearlessness. This moment last about 60 seconds before I was engulfed in a fear that was equally inexplicable and intense. Confusing, I know. Let me break it down. I was beginning to conceptualize that fear played a role in every decision I have ever made. Large or small, it played a part. From what the implications were, the future, the present, what needed to be done, how it was going to be done. Fear has played a role in every aspect of my life.

Feeling complete fearlessness took away one of the core foundations of how I've lived for more than two decades. I was not mentally prepared to live that way. Honestly, I'm still not. To have absolutely no regard for any outcome or any expectation on any situation in life. It is the ultimate surrendering of all control and I am just not ready for that. Nor have I ever met anyone in my life that has been able to do so. I was terrified at the thought of living without any fear. So I stopped arguing with God, for the moment, and knew that at the very least I needed to stop trying to control this process. I needed to stop trying to rush through all of the pain, attempting to cram my mid life crisis from months into hours. There was no shortcut here and I had to accept that. But I did receive a truly extraordinary gift.

I was slowly catching my breath again and began reflecting back to understand what happened. When the floodgates were open, I had screamed at God over and over again, "Why? Why? Why? Why did these things happen, why to a child, how could You?" And I finally got my answer, not through words but through feeling. Hurt people hurt people. For instance, I held so much resentment towards my father for dying. Forget the issues from my childhood, he could have quit smoking, he could have gotten the surgery to fix the clot in his leg, he could have done countless things that he didn't do. Instead, I would be left with a pain that could never be mended or healed. That was until I felt his pain. The agony he felt when he lost his family, when his sons chose to live with their mother over him, the loneliness, the shame, guilt and despair. He made so many mistakes. He didn't have friends for support, he didn't have religion, or read self help books or take classes or go and see a therapist. In fact, I hardly ever saw him smile or laugh my whole life. No, he wanted to die because death was easier than living with those burdens any longer. And for the first time I was not harboring hatred but empathy towards him and so many others that wounded me.

You see, it is easy to be angry. It is so much harder to forgive. Especially when that person personally hurt you or someone you love. But people do not wake up in the morning and wonder whose day they can ruin. We do not hurt people because we are so filled with joy all the time, and we are certainly not acting out of a place of love. No, we hurt people from our own pain. Hurt people hurt people. And we all have wounds, we are all hurting. It does not negate the fact that there are real consequences to those wounds, for us and for those around us. Even if we are so lucky that the wounds heal, there will still be scars left behind. They do not just go away. The difference is whether we live and act from our seeping wounds or we let them heal, we learn from them, and we live from our scars. Three years prior to all of this Kent gave a sermon at church about his time living in Israel during the holy wars. A suicide bomber blew up the café that he visited most days. Putting the picture of the gentleman up on the screen he talked about how easily that could have been him sitting in the café, leaving his wife and children behind. Yet instead of labeling this person as a terrorist, he gave one pressing question to the crowd; can you see this man not as a terrorist or a murderer, but as a nine-year-old boy that simply wants to play soccer with his friends?

We all start off as children, innocent and full of love. Pain, on the other hand, is cyclical, it is passed down, it is passed on. We are not taught how to bear it or how to handle it well. I believe the fear that comes with pain is a large reason why we pass it on. But when we can hold that pain, and face that fear, we have the opportunity to morph it into a gift. To see that other person drowning in their sorrow and respond not with more pain and more fear, but with grace, love and compassion. We need to take the opportunity to forgive because forgiveness is ultimately not about that person over there, it's about releasing us from the pain and fear that is controlling us from within. Just like with not taking anything personally, this is ultimately about our foundation of joy. We have the opportunity to end the cycle. The pain, the fear, can stop here.

CHAPTER 6 NOTES AND REFLECTIONS

What are some memories from your past that you still struggle with? Is there forgiveness you need, or need to give to someone else? Are you able to see yourself or that person in a different light?

7

ENDURING DESPAIR:

from losing weight to losing love, all you need is that P word, patience

Patience has never been my strong suit, in fact I don't know a whole lot of people that are really that good at it. After all this is our culture, we want the quick fix, we want the easy answers, and we want it now. Not tomorrow, yesterday. Let's pick on dieting for an easy example. When you are trying to lose weight, it sucks. Yet there is a multi-billion-dollar industry out there that glorifies the next big thing. I remember taking a clinical nutrition class where we studied why promises like, "the fat-fabulous ten-day diet that will melt the pounds off" don't work. What actually happens is you lose some water weight for a couple of weeks that comes right back, because your metabolic processes could not kick in fast enough to start burning fat (short of you starving yourself). We end up back at square one. We have magical pills that boost the metabolic process, until you read the fine print of the study, and suddenly it's not as exciting as the models on TV made it out to be. There is scientifically no such thing as magical pills or quick fixes for weight loss. It takes lifestyle changes, it takes eating a healthy diet and it takes lots of exercise. The biggest ingredient is patience. But as our culture demands instant gratification, it is no surprise most of us get frustrated and give up when we aren't instantly looking like Baywatch lifeguards jogging in slow motion down the grocery aisle at Whole Foods after two weeks at the gym let alone after two months. Eating one doughnut won't make you gain weight, but eating doughnuts every day for years on end will. We don't get out of shape overnight, we didn't gain or lose weight overnight, our health doesn't collapse overnight and we don't get to escape it overnight.

In most cases our fears did not come overnight, and we don't just get to walk away from them overnight. Most of us will walk away from the opportunity to face our fears long before we even scratch the surface. Most of us will give up after two weeks when we need to fight more than ever. I know I have dozens of times. Patience and I are not friends. We are getting there, but that's been a journey all on its own.

When I was told that I needed to have patience and sit in "the hard" to see what it was going to teach me, I never truthfully knew how long that was going to take. It's a good thing too, because had I known I'd be looking at many months, I would have walked away right then and there, just like I had always done in the past. In fact, it's a process I'm still learning from. Fear can manifest itself in many different ways, one of which is pain. If scientists are correct and loneliness registers in the same part of the brain as physical pain, then it's no wonder why sitting in "the hard" can be so agonizing. More often than not, we feel alone in our fears. Like no one would understand, so why even bother? We convince ourselves that we are isolated in our pain and it makes the sting of loneliness that much worse.

All of us are touched by the pain of love in some form or another. Whether it was losing a loved one, leaving someone, someone leaving you, being lied to or betrayed, love is a tricky, complicated beast. Having your heart broken can oftentimes be just as painful, if not more painful, than someone passing away. It seems strange, but when someone leaves you, they are making a conscious choice not to be with you. They still exist; they are just over there somewhere and you can't be with them. It torments the mind; you are constantly replaying memories, trying to figure out why and trying to resolve the past. In death, separation is permanent; there is no changing the situation and no unknowns in regard to the relationship. Like everything we talk about in this book, there are a million factors and combinations that come into play that change the context of this. What I really want to get across here is we tend to either downplay heartache or let it consume us. In both cases, we have to start by simply being vulnerable enough to acknowledge the pain, sit in it, and talk about what we are afraid of in the situation.

I'm not going to say it was a breeze, but losing the money, the companies, and facing my childhood was relatively easy compared to losing my family. I say this with a strong aside that losing all those things was terribly difficult; it turned my world upside down. However, losing my partner and our new family was significantly more painful. I could actively work to undo my past and take steps forward, money comes and goes, businesses can be rebuilt, but coming home to a house that is no longer a home is not something there is a quick fix for. This void can't just be filled even though we try to fill it in all sorts of ways.

Whether because of death or someone's choice, there are countless nights lying in bed tossing and turning while the mind races around the sun. On the off chance you get to sleep, you wake up to still find you are all alone — assuming your mind left your dreams to be at peace for once. It's agonizing, it tests every inch of your core and can consume you in your darkest moments. How many songs in every genre of music were written as the result of a broken heart? This is when escaping and numbing out almost feels vital to our survival. We will do anything for a breath, anything to not feel that sting, even if for only a moment. Unfortunately, no matter what we do, we can't take that sting away, and it returns because until we actually sit with it and learn from it, it isn't going anywhere.

What we find when we sit with the pain can often be the hardest part. Small or large, we all had a part to play in it. How do you sit with this reality, knowing that you could have caused someone else pain? Now there are always instances in which this doesn't apply, but for many of us, we play the victim. It was true for me when my partner left, when my father passed, and everything in between. This isn't easy to discuss and I know some of the knee jerk reactions that come from saying this. I also know what it's like to say, "But you don't understand." I'm going somewhere with this so try and ride this out with me for a moment. Playing victim is inevitably another form of escape. It is much easier to say, "Poor me," than ask the hard questions like, "What did I contribute"? For example, think about talking to your friends after a lover leaves you; what is their typical response? I would bet a shiny penny that you've heard or said one of these lines; you deserve better than him, he was a complete jerk; oh she was crazy you'll find someone better; I can't believe you liked him in the first place, you just need to meet "the one."

Our friends and family build walls to try and protect us. They don't tell us what we did wrong; on the contrary, they sharpen their axes and get ready to go to war for us. We love going to war over things, it is something that binds us together. When you hurt one of us, oh boy are you going to regret that! The result? Families divide, friends divide and houses divide. Here's the most unhelpful part about all of this; the focus is now off of your pain and your fears and your struggles and instead it is focused on someone or somewhere else. Whether that means buying you a drink, or many drinks, talking gossip about that other person, chick flicks, sad songs, pizza, chocolate, parties or finding the new magical "other," your pain gets pushed to the back of the line. It distracts you momentarily, which sometimes is definitely needed, but in the end it doesn't do anyone any good and it certainly doesn't help foster healing.

Don't become a harsh critic and don't get stuck. None of the previously mentioned examples should be used in the opposite extreme, to shame and guilt ourselves. We cheat on our diets and sometimes we need to just cry it all out when our heart is throbbing. This is not a bad thing; it's only when we let it define us that it controls us again. When we say we will never lose weight, I can't do it, and I will never love again, I will not open my heart, or I don't deserve to be happy and I don't deserve to be skinny. End all references to "I don't deserve," because you most certainly don't deserve to talk to yourself that way. Now remove love, remove diets and place whatever burden you are currently facing in its place — career, finances, friends, family, kids, projects, health etc. This cycle, this thought process pertains to so many aspects of our lives. Fear will keep the cycle going on to the next job, the next relationship or the next project and we will repeat the same mistakes all over again until we face it head on.

The reason why I tell you to challenge victimhood is not because people don't do and say terrible things, and not because we don't do and say terrible things to ourselves; to some extent we are all victims. But we cannot heal when we are stuck in victimhood, which gives away control and leaves us helpless. In relationships, we can't change that other person, we can't help them grow or learn from their mistakes, and they will face their own realities and struggles with their own consequences. But we can get a clearer understanding of the things we did wrong, how we contributed, and how we can have more control moving forward to engage life from a better, whole self. It won't ever be found in a magical other waiting to "complete us," because that magical other doesn't exist. The only person that can complete us is our self. We won't be whole when we lose ten pounds, buy that bigger house, or finish that back patio. Finding our whole self is not based on external measurements nor societal norms. We have to learn to breathe and try not to tackle the entire to-do list of patience in one bite.

Want to try and practice this change? A simple way to practice patience is to look at how we react in a disagreement, whether this be your boss, your spouse, a friend or your child. Sitting in "the hard" starts with the very basics. So when someone says something to you that upsets you, DON'T react, don't lash out, don't yell back, don't become passive aggressive or fall silent. Respectfully acknowledge that you heard what they said and request some time to think about it. The first time you try this you will be crawling in your skin. This will be harder than that day you ran out of time, skipped lunch and showed up to the rehearsal dinner where you conveniently had to walk past the table with mini cheesecakes to get to your seat. Do you want to wait another 45 minutes for some iceberg lettuce when you feel like Betty White in the Snickers commercial? Of course not! Give me a mini cheesecake ... or five.

It will take all of your willpower to not react, however you typically react. Take it home, write it down and stare at it, meditate on it, journal about it, talk out loud to yourself about it, whatever you need to do. If you don't get your inner anger out, you won't be able to focus, but the goal is to try and understand why it made your stomach churn the way it did. Start with a question like, what do you have to contribute to this situation? When we react in the moment, our heart rate increases, our blood pressure rises and our cognitive ability for emotional reasoning diminishes by the second. We get defensive or we attack, and in neither case will we be able to listen or comprehend the other's point of view. We will not see things from their perspective. This is where fights start, inner tensions boil and feelings get hurt. There is not growth in any of this, there is no healing in any of this. No one's voice, no matter how wrong or right, ignorant, disrespectful or full of grace will be heard, and thus no change will happen. No one will see things from a different point of view and it will all be a waste of time to keep stubborn egos intact.

When we react to whomever in whatever manner we react, they once again have control over our emotions. We are letting the actions of another dictate our happiness. When you are sitting with that anger and frustration ask yourself, "Is this life-giving to me?" We know reacting will not be life-giving to the other person, but I'm talking about you. Is it life-giving for you to nod and smile and then turn around and gossip behind that person's back? Is it life-giving to fight, or judge, or talk about that person in this way? After all, what is most life-giving for you will likely be what is life-giving for those around you and for the world. But it first starts with having patience and understanding the reaction in the first place. Don't forget the notion of not taking anything personally. The hard truth is that person, distasteful or not, is engaging or responding from a place of pain and fear themselves; why else would they do or say those things? In the statement that is all but overused yet under utilized, can you find yourself in their shoes?

All of this patience means we have to sit and face those fears that keep us from finding our whole self. The ones that ruin our diets, dismantle our relationships, and cause us to argue with anyone that disagrees with us. Until we find our whole self, we are going to keep searching for it in another person, another job with a new boss, in another place or in some object. It doesn't have to be this way; there are other steps we can take, together.

It's time to get to work.

CHAPTER 7 NOTES AND REFLECTIONS

How are you impatient? Are there areas in your life where you play the victim? Are there situations in which you can take a different look to ask what part you had to play in it?

PART 2

SURRENDERING TO THE FEAR

In a day filled with
joy, sadness, struggles and triumph,
may we never forget that
the best is yet to come.
So may we not take it for granted,
but be ever thankful
for all that life has
to offer here,
in this moment,
now

8

WALKING INTO THE DESERT:
our first step towards tangible change

"The thing one fears most, is fear." I've been carrying around this quote on a fortune cookie wrapper for six years now. If I were honest, I wish that I could say I came out of the woods that sunny, fall day and everything was fixed. Instead it was just the start. That was my first moment in life when I was truly taking a step towards entering the desert. The desert is our place of isolation where we are forced to face our inner fears, insecurities, pain and turmoil. Where it feels like the vital nutrients of our life don't exist and we are struggling just to survive the scorching days and the freezing nights without any food, water or shelter. The desert is where our struggles are the most vivid and escaping them is nearly impossible. The scariest part about entering the desert is that only you can enter it. Alone. Friends can support you, therapists can guide you, books can teach you, but only you can decide whether or not you are going to enter the desert. It's unique to only you and your story, which is why no one can walk it for you.

Historically, most societies, cultures and religions had some form of entering the desert. Girls and boys were sent into the woods, into the huts, on vision quests, fasting, 40 days and 40 nights, you name it - we were intentionally forced into the unknown to face our fears and wrestle with them. In our culture today, we go from elementary, to middle school, to high school, to getting a job or to college, then to starting a career, then to families, kids, and then twenty years of their school and supporting their cycle. There is no break, no time to be alone, and no time to find one's self. I think that's part of why people go to college and just let loose, drop out of school and travel the world, struggle with life choices, struggle with careers, struggle in relationships, and inevitably, struggle with themselves. After all, where does the midlife crisis stem from? It's not the only reason those things happen, but often times when people go on these journeys a common theme you hear is "I was finding myself" or "I'm discovering who I really am."

When things are going well in our lives, it's very uncommon to say, "Things are going so well, I think I need to change something." No, typically we decide things need to change when things are going all wrong. When we are lost, when pain consumes us and we decide we have had enough. Despair can be an incredibly powerful driving force in our lives. It is like a taxi dropping us off at the front gates of the desert. Here's the tricky part about the desert — there are no set rules for saying how long of a journey the desert will be, and I don't know if we ever truly go all the way through to the other side because everyone's deserts are different. There is so much unknown about it.

Another way to look at the desert is not as a one-time event with an end point but as a continuum that our life has.

On one side fear controls everything about your life, on the other side life is perfect and fear controls nothing. We will move back and forth depending on the storms and seasons of life, always striving to get closer to the other side. But we will fall back and we will need to enter the desert from time to time, like keeping in shape. The most grueling part is always the beginning, but after that you learn what works best for you and how to stay flexible. However, I think the most common theme I've seen and experienced in my own journey is that we tend to fall far short of ever actually entering into the desert in the first place, let alone walking through it or coming back out of it. One step on that scorching hot sand and we realize the perils this journey will have with no end in sight. We turn around and hop back in that taxi cab of despair and look for the nearest exit. Back to escaping we go.

Remember how we all hold those PhDs in escaping our fears? This is where escaping comes out the strongest. When we lose the labels that define our lives, we have a chance to redefine what our lives means, what is actually important to us. We have the opportunity to create labels that matter the most to our inner being, not necessarily what our parents, friends or society told us we needed to label our selves with. This means confronting those "shoulds" and "oughts" in our lives that guilt and shame us into staying stuck. Perhaps you lose your job and the quickest response after a night of binge drinking is to run out and find another job. Or you go through a breakup and the quickest way to end the pain is to jump back into another relationship. The title of an accountant, or a wife is important, yes, but it does not define who you are at your core, because you are more than just what you do for a living or who you are married to. We do not give ourselves time to process why that relationship was hard in the first place, or the things we did or didn't like about that job. We do not give ourselves time to process whether we even wanted to be an accountant in the first place. Many of us try to relive the glory days, getting lost in nostalgia. Sports cars, parties, fancy trips, entertainment, adventure, watching TV and sports, anything to avoid walking into that desert. How we avoid it or what the desert even looks like can be different for all of us, but why we avoid it also seems to have a common theme.

The desert is where all of the fears come to life. This is no longer about getting upset at a friend for saying that thing, this is understanding why we got upset in the first place. This is where we face our thing behind our thing, this is where we go to battle. The problem with this situation is the longer we wait, the more armor, castles and walls we have reinforced our fears with. We thought we were keeping the fear contained, but in reality we were arming it to stay in control of our lives permanently (like the caged beast metaphor). When we enter the desert we become the peasants with pitchforks charging the armed castle gates. If we surround the castle long enough, we will chip away at its foundation, and ultimately bring the walls crashing down, but this will be a test of determination. You have to give yourself grace here because you are going to stumble and fall, bruise your knees and scrape your elbows more times than you can count. If it were easy, not only would everyone have done it already, but the world would be this perfect peaceful place. Escaping is easy, facing the pain is not.

My friends Sarah and Jon had a kid unexpectedly at a young age. The natural tendency, as influenced by much of the culture in Western Michigan, is to immediately settle down and get married. That's just what they did and even chose to have a second child. Absolutely beautiful girls, but like all families, they had their struggles. Sarah is one of those women filled with compassion. Now I don't want to ever paint anybody with the brush of perfection as that's not fair to Sarah; we all have our faults and we are all imperfect. But Sarah was one of those people who, no matter how hard of a day she was having, she was always going to ask you about yours. It was hard to see Sarah when Jon decided one day that this was not the life he wanted. He disappeared overnight, drained the bank account, and went out to relive the days he lost — and I don't have to go into detail with what that entails. He wanted nothing to do with their children and it devastated her.

What do you say to a single mother of two, attempting to make sense of such deep despair when she can't afford to pay her bills, the kids constantly ask where daddy is, and the man she thought she would spend her life with was now in the arms of another woman? It's one of those stories in which she's trying her best just to survive and her best to love her children, but then the car breaks down, and getting the kids to school or making it to work takes on a whole new meaning of struggle. By the grace of another she's finally able to get another vehicle... weeks later someone hits her on the road and wrecks the new vehicle. It was a consistent theme in everything she faced. It's not even necessary to point out that she was drowning and life just kept kicking her in the face. Accepting help was almost all but out of the question because Sarah believed it was her fault that she was in this situation. She didn't believe that she even deserved help and was consumed by the guilt and shame, even the embarrassment upon accepting help. Honestly, sometimes help can be painful too.

I remember taking Sarah's girls out to the zoo one day and having an absolute blast. We went and got them groceries, even ended it by watching Frozen and eating tasty treats. What more could a four and six-year-old ask for? It was great for the girls, for us, and for Sarah. Sometimes though, even joy in those moments can be painful because, as much fun as it was, Sarah actually wished it was someone else she was sharing those memories with. The person she meant to spend her life with, not another figure who can't actually fill that role. It can create a temporary distraction from the pain, but not a permanent one. After the fun day is over and the kids are off to bed, loneliness returns, that sting of not having someone next to you to share the burdens and joys of life with.

I want to pause the story here and ask a simple question. How much anger and blame do you have for Jon? How many of you can relate, or know a friend in a similar situation and just want to reach through the book and give him a piece of your mind? Here is where we get to practice grace. He did not walk away from his family because he was loving life and wanted to cause someone else pain. He walked away because he was struggling deeply and fear consumed him. Remember this is not about justifications but the truth that hurt people hurt people. It was hard to see him and not feel deep resentment and a desire to judge, but I can promise you that he was stuck in his own hell that no night of fun could replace. He will have forever hurt people he loved and cared about and there are deep consequences for his actions that can be forgiven, but not forgotten.

It takes grace to remember that there is always more than meets the eye and it takes even more grace and humility to not judge another for the mistakes they made, no matter how big or small. Ultimately, if we cannot forgive another person for their mistakes, if we cannot give them grace, how on earth are we ever going to forgive and give ourselves grace for the mistakes we have made and will continue to make for the rest of our lives? Sometimes walking into the desert and facing all of our own fears and faults can make it infinitely easier to forgive and have compassion on others.

At the end of that day, fun and joy are still escapes from a pain that an ice cream cone and lion exhibit can't solve. It doesn't mean though, that knowing someone else cares about you doesn't give a little bit of strength to say, "I can make it through one more day," even when you don't want to. Sarah's walk in the desert would take years, and so would her partner's. Kids complicate things, age complicates things, life complicates things, and it can all extend our duration in the desert. But eventually, if we allow it, we will get through it and find joy when we never thought it was possible. Once we are able to let go of the parameters and labels that limit our joy, we are able to discover, or we are forced to discover the joy that actually comes from within — not given to us by someone or something else. When it comes from someone else, it can be taken away. By circumstance or choice, joy based on external factors will always inevitably fail us. To take this one step further, when that external factor fails, joy is never found in a greener pasture somewhere else.

I can't tell you how much greener pastures have affected the decisions in my life. We often refer to grass being greener on the other side when it comes to relationships, but it affects all aspects of our lives. Whenever things get hard, it is so much easier to say that this is simply not working and walk away. The problem with walking away when things get tough, the problem with walking out of the desert when your throat gets thirsty and your feet get hot, is that it will never solve anything. You will end up constantly looking for greener pastures in everything. Relationships, jobs, projects, friends, you-name-it are all replaceable. But every one and every thing comes with its own set of difficulties and its own set of indifferences.

Even if it looks greener, I can confidently say that it is not. Although it may look gorgeous and lush right now, at some point the rains will slow down, it will get hot, and the grass will turn brown again. That's when we tend to decide to move elsewhere, like the grazing animals of the prairie, instead of waiting for the rain to return. The problem with migration is, you never get to sit still and you never get to settle. My mother once said to me that the grass may not always be greener elsewhere, but there is such a thing as soil that is more fertile. I don't deny that, it is true that certain jobs are easier and certain people you may get along better with. But I'm also a natural resource management major by trade, and I can promise you that it is possible to turn barren, rocky, sandy soil into a lush, thriving field. Whether you think you are the barren soil, or some one, some place, or some thing else is barren, with enough patience and cultivation of compassion and grace you can find yourself standing barefoot in a field of boundless beauty. It is all based on your perception, one of the few things over which you do have control. How do you know what field you should be standing in? When you walk through the desert and find yourself you will either know, or even more likely realize that it doesn't matter. No field will bring you joy or make you whole, only you can do that. Fields are only meant to add to the already existing joy you have.

When I did a ten-day meditation workshop with Headspace, founder Andy Puddicombe shared a really great example of finding that joy within. He related joy to standing on the earth under a clear blue sky. Life always has some clouds that can enter our days, which for the most part are ok. But sometimes those clouds get really dark, they fill the sky, and torrential downpours happen with lightning striking all around us. The hard part to remember when you are trying survive the storm is that just above those clouds, just above that storm, that blue sky is still there with the sun shining just as brightly as the day when life seemed to be grand. We all have the potential within us to get back to that blue sky because the storm is a guarantee in life and this too shall pass.

I don't want to imply that letting go of those labels that define you in order to walk through the desert and face these storms will be synonymous with finding all new labels. It's not to say some of your current labels won't still be the exact same after the desert as they were before, but hopefully, there will be another shift in perception. The clouds and storms of life will always come. Life will always have difficulties, there will always be more stress and more unexpected turbulence. But they don't have to control us, they don't have to define us, and they don't have to determine our joy. When we can change our mindset from "I have to" or "I should do this" into "I get to do this," the storms are no longer in control of you. You get to dictate how you respond and how much it will ultimately add to or detract from your joy.

If you are willing to have patience and sit in the hard and avoid the tendency to escape or seek greener pastures, you then have the strength to enter into the desert and face all of the fears that are holding you back. If you can get through the desert, your life will be forever changed, and I hope in the following chapters I can share some of the wisdom I've been given on how to make it through to the other side and find the blue skies that are always there whenever we are ready to access them again.

CHAPTER 8 NOTES AND REFLECTIONS

Have you ever tried to "find yourself"? What has been your version of the desert(s)? What are your greener pastures?

9

FEAR OF FEAR, ITSELF (desert continued):

defining "enough" to build a foundation for joy, not happiness

When I began writing this book, I was four chapters in when my laptop was stolen. This was not a scenario in which I left my car unlocked with the laptop sitting on the dashboard and a sign saying "please take me." No, this was the middle of the day; someone entered my friend's apartment while we were there, walked past the dog, cut a hole through the screen door and strolled right in while we were ten steps away. I heard a noise and went into the room seconds later to find it gone. I didn't have my iCloud set up properly so it turns out I not only lost the book, but a decade of photos. All of my passwords, banking info, tax documents, work documents, you-name-it were right there in the open. The complex's cameras were phony and someone swiped my computer before I could lock it out, leaving all my information open to take. Now, I've never been one to constantly lock my house or car because there are few things I held of dear value and the rest I didn't want to stress over. My computer, on the other hand, I guarded with my life. It was all of my work and personal information and that thing was never out of my sight.

I was so caught up in writing this book and what I had lost that I spent hours desperately figuring out how to track down my computer, from the police to Craigslist to pawn shops. In my frantic search, I completely disregarded my friend and the invasion of her privacy that had taken place. She had just lost all sense of comfort and security where she lived and spent most of the day in tears, searching for a new place to live. She had lost the ability to sleep safely at night, to leave her doors unlocked or use her screen door in the dead of a sweltering Michigan summer. I didn't even consider the impact it was having on her until that day was almost over and my own fears had subsided. When I came back to reality, I felt ashamed, pathetic even.

I'm not saying I didn't lose something valuable because I did; I can't get those photos back. But what did I really lose? I still have my health, my daughter, they didn't steal all my money, I can rewrite this book (obviously) and photos can't replace the memories or experiences. My life will actually move on. It was not based on an electronic gadget no matter how valuable it was. Instances like these, when we get caught up in our own pain and anger, can make it really hard to see the pain of those around us. It places a veil over our eyes and not in a good way. One of the unique challenges in these situations, especially when we are deep in the desert and looking at fears, is to stop and question what the long-term impact of this moment is.

What will my life be like in ten days, ten months, how about in ten years? Was it frustrating that my laptop was still gone after ten days? Of course. But here is where we get to change our perspective on things. That laptop is a materialistic item; it can be replaced. I don't know that person's story, I don't know what drove them to steal my laptop in the first place. Is it possible that they had addiction issues? Knowing the area, it is a good possibility. But what if that person was raised in a traumatic household, whose father abused him? What if her mother told her she would never amount to anything? What if it was a kiddo who lived with a single mother and she could not afford to pay the bills and he thought if he could somehow make some money then he could help? What if that person was never told that they were loved or that they mattered? What if they never knew peace or grace in their life?

You see, we tend to jump to conclusions when we don't know the story. Fear consumes us and our reaction is to get angry, to judge and to condemn anyone that affects us negatively. But while we are getting lost in these negative emotions, we lose our ability to see beyond the veil. When I was consumed with anger, I lost all ability to have empathy and compassion for someone who was likely struggling much harder in life than I was. Like hurt people hurting people, people don't steal because life is so perfect at home and they are free from financial or mental struggles, or from addictions. I also lost the chance to have empathy for my friend. I got to go home that night and sleep in a bed that was safe in a home that was not violated earlier that day. I lost out on an opportunity for compassion, an opportunity to be there for someone close to me in need. This is where it is so crucial to take the next step into the desert. Finding joy as your foundation, not happiness.

I've found when we are controlled by searching for happiness, we are constantly afraid of losing it. Happiness is momentary. It is a state of being that comes and goes, it fluctuates from ecstatic to non-existent. For example, if someone comes up to tell you that you look great in that new dress, it might put a smile on your face. If your boss tells you that you did a good job on this presentation, you might pat yourself on the back. If you've ever listened to the radio when that caller wins $1,000, there is always that one guy who responds, "Oh, thanks." But if you're anything like me, you're that person screaming at 100 decibels and you can't quite tell if it's a girl or a guy. It is safe to say that these things make you happy. After all, who does not like a free $1,000 check, recognition at work, or a nice compliment? But these things are just that, they are things. Things can be taken away from you in a moment's notice. You could take that $1,000 and buy a new laptop that someone steals the next day, that boss that complimented you could be the same one letting you go next week, and Jessica from sales may tell you that your shoes don't match your dress, whatever that means.

When happiness is derived from outside of oneself, it can be an addiction. It will point us back towards fear of fear itself. What if I'm not good looking enough, what if I don't make enough money, what if I don't do enough, what if I'm not a good enough parent or a good enough spouse, what will other people think of me? We become afraid of all of these potential fears and they then control our daily actions. We spend an hour getting ready for work and skip breakfast to try and look pretty enough. We wear an entire stick of deodorant to stop the perspiration while standing in front of the person we are desperately trying to please. And no matter how much money we make, it is never enough because what if x, y or z happens. Or I really need to purchase this, this, and this in order to be satisfied, in order to be happy.

I say this as someone who has done these things myself and witnessed the trail of destruction it left in my life. Instead of calling it fear of fear itself, another way to think about it is our addiction to social media. Have you ever hopped on Facebook and started scrolling only to realize you just lost twenty minutes of your day staring at pictures of everyone else's day? It is easy to doctor anything up and post it on Facebook to paint the picture-perfect life. It especially gets addicting when friends and family start commenting and liking your posts and it is also an easy place to start playing the comparison game; all emotional reasoning is now lost.

Our brains are wired towards negativity. It's why we can receive 99 positive emails and one negative email and spend all day focused on that one sour email we got. I've felt this on social media when I post my vacation pictures of Florida, but Steve went to Greece. Why am I not good enough, cool enough, or rich enough to take my family or friends to Greece? I should be in Greece! It's also how we can watch a video of a kid sharing his last moment with cancer, we can be crying over our phones, and not even two minutes later be giggling watching a cat video. Now I do realize platforms like Facebook can be great tools to keep in touch with family and friends, or that it can be used to promote awareness and education. But I've seen how "education" can be translated into judgments and hate, and I've seen how "keeping in touch" is an excuse to avoid actually taking the time to reach out to someone. How deeply connected do you feel at the end of the day to your hundreds or thousands of Facebook friends or Instagram and Snapchat followers? These platforms create fleeting moments of connection that do not really exist because you cannot sit with me in my pain and despair simply because you put a sad face on my post. You cannot share in the intimate joy of my kid's birthday party over "liking" a picture. It's momentary and very volatile. Happiness is like scrolling on social media, it comes, it goes, and it is dependent on external factors and outside influences. Joy comes from within.

> I would define "happiness" as a temporary feeling of pleasure or contentment. I would define "joy" as being filled with pleasure or contentment.

The more we release the control of fear on our lives and our decisions, the more accessible joy becomes. Joy is not a temporary state, it cannot be take away from us and it is not altered by the outside world. This does not mean that we don't have moments in our life when joy persists more than other times, but think about joy and happiness like a tree. The branches and leaves are happiness in our life, storms come and break branches, seasons change, leaves may die and fall to the ground, spring may bring new life back to us. But joy is our roots, joy is what supplies the life to the branches and leaves, joy is what helps us weather the storm. Without a strong foundation in joy, without good roots, we are blown over by the first gust of wind that comes our way. Building good roots takes more time and more patience. The stronger your roots become, the more branches you can support. The more branches you can support, the more life you will be able to offer into this world in the very air we need to breathe; compassion, grace and love.

A question that comes up is, "How do we identify true joy?" The answer is like most things, you test it. Sometimes the storms in life never seem to let up. At other times it seems like things are calm and we get comfortable. We all get comfortable and feel like our work is done, or we do not have to work anymore. Sometimes when life gets calm we walk away from the desert, or believe we really don't need to go in in the first place. But this only lasts as long as life stays calm, and we all know the storms eventually return. In either case, it can be really hard to work on your foundation when your world is flipping upside down just like it can be hard when we get complacent and think everything is fine. When our foundation is not rooted in joy we are more prone to respond to all difficult situations with more anger, judgment and condemnation. We always need to work on our joy as the foundation to our wellbeing. Then the more it is tested, the more we can respond with grace, love and compassion. This too is a continuum, not an end point. The more we work at it, the stronger it becomes, and the more capable we become at offering ourselves grace when we make mistakes and stumble.

CHAPTER 9 NOTES AND REFLECTIONS

Are you searching for happiness or building a foundation for joy? What brings you joy? Reflect on when difficult things in life happen; are you able to react calmly and see a bigger picture or do you get tossed about like a plastic bag in a wind storm?

10

SURRENDER:

does joy exist in despair?

I remember the first time I had to go in for a scan at the hospital, laying on that hard table staring up at the ceiling. Those rooms have picturesque tiles in the ceiling of sunsets, butterflies or fishing trips, trying to help calm the anxious mind. It is pleasant, yes, but it did not truthfully detract from the contrast IV that is about to be inserted into my arm. I was afraid and doubts began to fill my mind. Sometimes I get consumed with doubt, and not just the small doubts like, "Is this going to work or not," but the big doubts. I doubt my purpose in life, I doubt the purpose of any of this, period. So what do I say to someone when they are waiting on the call from the doctor or they do not know how they are going to pay their bills? To a woman who cannot bear children or a teenager who no longer wants to live in this life? When a spouse confesses that he or she has doubts about the marriage working or to a mother holding her dying child? When I'm struggling, the last thing I want to hear is someone say, "it will all be ok," or "don't worry, be happy." This feels like putting picturesque tiles in the ceiling of a hospital room. Of course it will be ok, but it is not ok right now and I am not living for tomorrow. And the blind optimism of "don't worry, be happy," does not pay my bills, cure cancer or fix relationships. But trying to control the struggle or fight against it will not help either. It takes an element of surrendering our attempts to try and control, cover up or avoid all of the pain in our lives and in this world.

First off, I want to make it clear that I don't have the answers and I do not know if they even exist. I don't know why Jessica's daughter got cancer and passed away. I don't know why Jim's sole purpose in Vietnam was to collect the dead bodies of his friends. I don't know why I held Melanie's hand at 38 years old as she said goodbye to her four children and husband. I don't why tsunamis wipe out villages, millions die from famine or why a billion people have no access to clean water when I get to sit in a state surrounded by clean water, fair weather and ample food supplies. But here is what I do know; every trial I have ever faced, every painful story I listened to from another, have all taught me something if I was willing to sit with it and embrace the emotion — not fight against it. There is an external reaction to events and there is also an internal reaction when we bottle it up and it eats away at us. If you want to be mad, give yourself permission to be mad; if you want to scream at the heavens, scream at the heavens; if you want to collapse and weep uncontrollably, give yourself permission to cry. Trying to cover it all up or lying to yourself or others will only make it worse.

Once we can learn to surrender and sit with our pain, as well as the pain of others, it can stop the knee-jerk reactions and gives us the opportunity to decide how to react. It means we get to choose whether this pain will rob us of our joy or our opportunity to have grace, compassion and love for another. Archbishop Desmund Tutu describes the atrocities of an issue like Syria's civil war. But he also talks about the other side of the equation with the countless humans who are called to serve; from Doctors without Borders to the White Helmets to those helping refugees feel safe in a new distant country. If I asked you what percentage of your life is difficult, painful, or shadowed by grief where happiness was all but nonexistent what would you tell me? 10%, 25%, maybe 50%, even 75%? Let's say your life is 50/50, meaning half the time you are pretty happy and half the time you are facing a struggle of some kind, from work to relationships to kids to your health to just life in general. Walking through the desert and finding a new foundation is about finding joy not just when life is going well but also when life is not, to ensure that half of your life is not wasted. But can joy really exist in despair?

Take a moment to ask yourself if most or all fear is valid. If you look back ten years, or five years, even five weeks ago, was it good for you to let that fear (big or small) control you? That fear that ruined that day or perhaps ruined many days? Or did things turn out ok? I know that not everything turns out ok, we lose chances, there are inexcusable things that happen, we make many mistakes and we have all grieved the death of a loved one whose time came too soon. But you are here in this moment now, reading this, which means you have made it this far. Every breath you take is a gift of life that you are not physically in control of, and every one of us will have our last breath on this earth. So what stops us from living in the moment now?

I think more often than not we wait for joy to come to us. I know I personally have made my joy circumstantial. When I get the right job, make enough money, have the perfect family, my body is fit, my kid graduates, when I stop making mistakes, when the storms of life end, etc. When we get angry or hurt or scared, we shut the world out and the joy with it. When we don't get that perfect job or the love of our life leaves or we mess up yet again or we lose it all, we scream, "What is the point?!" We ask why, we don't believe or don't want to believe in a purpose, we don't understand and we certainly don't want to be happy. Doubt can return to consume us and we lose any chance of finding joy in despair again.

—Finding joy <u>in</u> all things, not <u>for</u> all things—

Finding joy in despair does not discount struggle and pain in present or old wounds. No, finding joy in despair is about changing the perception on the fear that is controlling us in the dark times. It's being able to weep with a friend at a funeral for the loss of a loved one while simultaneously being grateful for all the joy they brought into your life. It's sitting with someone when their world is falling apart to say, I'm going to be here for you when you can barely see through the pain. The path of joy is looking at a broken world filled with broken people and choosing to see the goodness that lies in everyone. It is when we sit with that really hard struggle and ask what it has to teach us, instead of letting it rob us of the moment we have now.

I admitted Tim to the hospital at 54 years old when he had an intestinal rupture. The doctors said it would kill him to operate so the only option left for him was to refuse all food and fluids by mouth to prolong his life for as long as he could. I took care of Tim and his family for the next four days and seeing his smile always brightened my day. On my last shift that week, it was going to be Tim's last night. It was nothing short of a miracle that he came back to consciousness when I entered the room that night to say goodbye to the family. I stood there holding Tim's hand in mine. I could tell in his eyes he knew that when he went back to sleep he would not likely wake up again. As he began to cry he looked at me whispering "thank you" over and over again. I looked around to see the immense pain in every family member and to his wife who could not fathom life without her partner. It was gut wrenching and emotionally exhausting to say goodbye, but I was so grateful to be a part of his final days, to be a part of a man's story who taught me that joy could not only exist amidst such agonizing despair, but it could flourish.

Whatever the trial is that you are facing, no matter how simple or earth-shattering it is, you are not alone. But if you cannot sit with it and see what it has to teach you, it will likely consume you instead. If you are able to sit with it and ask those questions, then it is possible to find an immense joy full of compassion and gratitude, even in your final days.

CHAPTER 10 NOTES AND REFLECTIONS

Do you need help finding joy in despair and are you willing to admit that to someone? Do you have extra joy you may be able to share with someone else and how could you do that? What would surrender look like to you?

11

LETTING GO OF OUTCOMES AND EXPECTATIONS:

entering the desert, one way or another we have to let go

I remember some of the first people I sat with while walking through my desert. The scenarios were always completely random. People ten, twenty, thirty years older than I sharing their life story, and by the end of the conversation asking me for guidance or input. These conversations were always intense and the stories these wonderful people would share were often filled with such pain and despair. I was grateful to even be a part of it. However, at the end of every discussion I could not help but feel queasy. The thought would run through my head over and over again, "Who am I to give advice or offer input, I am too young." What could I possible know after all?

By the time my pastor AJ had asked me if I'd be willing to share my story at church in the spring of 2017, I was really getting uncomfortable. The question now morphed into, "What could I possibly have to offer to the world?" What I really wanted to tell him was to call me in thirty years. Then one night I was reading Rob Bell's book, *How to Be Here*, and he talked about this swirling question we use on ourselves, "Who am I to ______?" The response was simple — if you have been through a storm, if you have learned something, if you have gained some wisdom in life, who are you not to share that gift back with the community? I personally think the older we get, the more life experience we receive, and the more gifts we acquire to offer back to the community. But young and old alike, we all have gifts to offer. If you don't believe me, take a child for a hike in the woods. Watch how they will open your eyes to all of the birds, insects and flowers. They will force you to walk slowly, to notice all of the beauty and abounding life all around you that you would normally race past.

That night I began writing what I would want to say if I shared my story. What I wanted to say became pages, pages broke into sections, sections became chapters and chapters became this book. To be fair, it took months, but here is the twist - when you write something that you are going to potentially share or make public, you put it back out there for the world to judge, to criticize and scrutinize. It's terrifying. People might disagree with me, people might attack me for the words in this book, but these words may also help someone else who really needs them. I'm a fan of cheesy quotes and one of my favorites is, "Stop trying to please everybody, you're not chocolate" (anonymous). Now this is not a get-out-of-jail-free card to do and say whatever you want. There is no need for more judgments or prejudice in this world on any level. But even when you are truly doing your best, even if you are trying so hard just to help, you have to let go of the outcomes and expectations. They will do one of two things; keep you from taking that chance and trying to help in the first place, or keep you from taking a second chance when things don't go quite the way you planned.

What are your "what ifs" in life? If you don't take a chance, you don't have to face them. What if I don't get the job? What if I ask her to marry me and she says no? What if it ends in a divorce? What if I invest and lose it all? What if my kid doesn't make the team? What if I fail? What if I get hurt, again? What if it all goes wrong? Fill in your blank; what if ________? Yes, all those things could happen, but what if it goes ok? What if it goes right? What if it becomes something beyond your wildest dreams? What if you end up marrying her? What if you end up running that company? What if you end up saving a life? What if you travel the world? What if that mistake grows up to say, "I love you mommy"? None of us know for certain what our risks will bring us, good or bad.

I was lucky enough to meet Don Schoendorfer who founded Free Wheelchair Mission (FWM). Don went on a mission retreat with his church to Morocco a decade ago where he noticed a shortage of mobility for any persons living with disability. Now this is a man who retired after spending decades engineering medical technology to save lives in hospitals across the world. It is safe to say Don could have hung his hat up and moved to a beach with a mojito as he'd contributed a lot to this world already. But he couldn't and he didn't. He saw a need and he knew he had a skill to offer. Don started with building three wheel chairs that he returned to Morocco with to hand out. I would not do it justice to retell the story of the woman chasing Don through the crowds as they loaded on to the bus, begging him to take a cup of water. It was all the family could offer but out of sheer gratitude they wanted to bless Don with a gift, any gift.

While the story is amazing, the dark reality for this issue is that Don discovered a demand for almost one hundred million wheelchairs worldwide. So Don got to work. FWM now builds extremely durable, lightweight, heavy-duty wheelchairs meant for rugged conditions in third world countries for the poorest of the poor. Easy to fix, easy to maintain with local parts, FWM can ship a wheelchair across the globe and have it delivered and assembled for well under $100 each. Here in the United States we can spend hundreds to thousands to get a competing wheelchair that would not last one month in the same conditions. FWM just celebrated giving away their one-millionth free wheelchair. One single man, with one single purpose, has solved 1% of a global issue with a small group of employees and the inspiration of thousands of dedicated volunteers and donors. Don said it was hard for him to celebrate this astonishing accomplishment because all he could focus on was how they would get wheelchairs to the next 99 million.

Don had lots of "what ifs". He also had lots of setbacks and struggles and admitted there was never an end goal or expectation in sight. He didn't cling to an outcome to create one hundred or one million wheel chairs. Instead, he simply saw a need and tried to do his best to be a part of the solution. He set his "what ifs" aside and decided to focus on how to take a step forward. That's how you impact a million lives. That's how a "what if" can grow beyond your wildest dreams.

Clinging to outcomes and expectations are vices that keep us stuck and bury us in our "what ifs." I think most of us are really good at either making the end result look like a fairy tale, or we end up seeing the worst in everything. Either situation sets us up for failure and disappointment. If it turns out short of a fairy tale, we feel cheated. Or, even if it's better than our worst imaginations, we will have spent the entire time waiting for it to go south and never actually enjoy it in the moment. Forgive me if country music isn't your cup of tea, but there is a beautiful song called "The Dance" by Garth Brooks. Whenever I'm in a hard spot it's on my go to list. He sings about being grateful for not knowing how it would end, because he could have missed the pain, but he also would have missed the dance. I think there is truth in that if we knew how hard some things were, we would avoid them entirely. We would avoid second, and third, and fourth chances too. A friend once told me having a kid was the best and worst thing that would ever happen to me. It's true that some of my hardest moments have come from having a child, but also some of my most cherishable moments have come from that bundle of love. I never would have guessed that to be true had I held on to my own outcomes and expectations.

Holding on to outcomes and expectations steals us away from the present moment. It is another form of fear trying to control what cannot be controlled. You can offer someone help and they can say no. You can give a kid a gift and she could cry. I don't think anyone ever gets married and plans that they will be getting a divorce a few years later. My first therapist buried two of her three children. One died in infancy, another died from an overdose in his late twenties. I could never imagine the pain she faced on a daily basis but she would remind me that she would choose to have her children all over again if she could. She had her days, we all have our days, but she chose to turn that pain into a gift to serve others and help people like me in my struggles. She wouldn't have been able to relate to my journey had she not been able to engage her own. This is true for all of us. If we cannot face our own struggles, we can never adequately have empathy and compassion for another and their struggles.

Our perception on death and dying may be one of the largest outcomes and expectations we cling to, or do everything in our power to avoid. I remember reading in *Kisses by Katie* about the difficulties of creating an orphanage in Africa, and everything she had seen, was going through and had sacrificed to get there. One lesson she taught me that sticks with me today is that most Christians talk about Lazarus being raised from the dead and what a miracle it was. What we don't talk about is the fact that if he was raised from the dead, he would have eventually grown sick and passed away again. From the minute we are born, we are dying. We all have a limited amount of time here on this earth. It's a struggle we all share and fight tooth and nail to delay. For some of us it is definitely shorter than others, but there is a difference in the reality of living for tomorrow or living from yesterday versus living in this moment now. We all know that death is inevitable, but it can also be a gift that gives life meaning in the present — if we let it.

It doesn't take much to derail us from this meaning though. The notions of what others will think, how this project will end, what will happen to me, how do I not repeat the past, how do I make this work; these thoughts can consume us. You wake up every morning and your lungs fill with air while your heart simultaneously beats. You eat food that other organisms in your intestines turn into energy to keep you moving forward. One hundred billion cells in your body die every single day and are replaced every single day. All of these things happen without your consent, without your control, without you saying so. They are gifts. One hundred, billion, gifts, a day, every day.

Funerals can be blunt reminders of how precious these gifts are. Especially when loved ones are gathered together and reminded of how short life is and how much our life matters through the pain. But I believe we dishonor the deceased when we go home and return to our daily routines to numb out the rest of our lives once more. We get momentarily caught up in these moments but they quietly fade away.

Have you ever noticed all of the calls, the love and the embraces during weeks surrounding someone's death? Speaking from personal experience, the 300th "I'm sorry for your loss" does not feel any different than the 3rd. In those moments, pain and fear is consuming and it's hard to be present when you are distracted by the presence of so many people. But after the moment fades away and everyone returns to their lives, that familiar sting of loneliness returns and it feels almost as though everyone else's life has moved on but yours. I don't need a hug on the day of the funeral, I need a hug two months later when everyone forgot that a funeral ever happened... it's like soup kitchens on Thanksgiving. Ask any soup kitchen and they will assure you that they do not need any more volunteers on Thanksgiving because it's the one day when everyone decides to volunteer. It's the 364 other days of the year when no one is looking that they need help.

Letting go of outcomes and expectations affects us not only in the hard places where fear is grappling around every corner, but it can also control how we engage in the positive. There is nothing wrong with feeling pleasure in serving another person, but when our motivations are based upon how it will end, benefit us, or how others will perceive it, we have failed before we started. Have you ever given someone a gift only to find out that they re-gifted it to another? Have you ever gone above and beyond to help someone and they wouldn't lift a finger for you in return? Have you ever spent hours making dinner for someone and they get up and walk away without so much as helping with the dishes or saying thank you? It's hard not to feel offended or take it personally, it's hard not to be upset or angry. But if we were only trying to be nice expecting something in return, it puts a couple things in motion. First off, it can be manipulative because you are trying to do something for a specific response out of a person. Secondly, it sets up other people to have control over our happiness again because it is dependent upon their response. Neither scenario lets us remain in control of our fate or allow us to engage the world from a foundation of joy.

Furthermore, serving someone with expectations can become a slippery slope when we start asking questions around the word "deserve." "Do they deserve it?" or "Do I deserve it?" are two more questions that will keep us stuck. This now means we are creating complex math equations around shame and guilt to decide the toxic question of who is worthy. Instead, the better question we can practice asking is, "Are they doing the best they can?" Maybe, maybe not. But once you feel comfortable at least taking the opportunity to say you might not know everything going on with that person in their life, even if it's your best friend, then you can turn the question back onto yourself; am I doing the best that I can?

This is how we get back to our foundation, this is how we take one step further away from letting outcomes and expectations control us. It's no longer about what friends or society think, how long we have to live, about our "what ifs," or what we will get in return. It comes down to how you perceive yourself. Whether it's your spouse of fifty years, or a person in the checkout line at the grocery store you will never see again, you have the opportunity to serve that person the best you can. You have the chance to make that single interaction an interaction they will remember. An interaction to bring a little bit more light into this world. You will no longer have to sit around and wonder "What if I have a heart attack tomorrow"? It becomes irrelevant simply because you are making the best of what you have today. This then releases you from the fear that keeps you from taking that leap or serving that person or taking that chance in the first place. You could smile at that person in line and they could tell you to turn around, you could bake your spouse a birthday cake and they could still leave you tomorrow, but at the very least, you will have engaged it with your all, from your authentic place, from who we were all meant to be in this world - a source of love, grace and compassion

When we let the mistakes of our past define who we are today, it will control our future. When we let fears and outcomes define our future, it controls the present moment. My business and all of my social programs blew up in my face. But I took a chance, I learned and I met countless amazing people along the way. If we all stopped moving after our first rejections then we'd all be single, we'd all be jobless, and we'd all be living in caves. So let's set the outcomes and expectations aside for a moment and take a chance on living life again.

In the words of Garth Brooks, "Our lives are better left to chance, I could have missed the pain. But I'd have to miss the dance."

CHAPTER 11 NOTES AND REFLECTIONS

What are your "what ifs"? What outcomes and expectations keep you stuck? What are you afraid of going horribly wrong? What would happen if it went horribly right?

12

WHEN ENOUGH REALLY IS ENOUGH:

engaging vulnerability to redefine "enough"

I want to share one of my largest false perceptions that I've carried much of my life; first world problems do not compare to the rest of the world. I was always a firm believer that we, as Americans, do not know true struggle and we do not know what "enough" is. For example, our average grocery store boasts 47,000 choices of food to purchase. We have fruits and vegetables available year round from all corners of the world. So how could we know true hardship as twenty million people face famine in Sub-Saharan Africa as I write this book? There are countless examples of unimaginable hardships, but many of them come with valuable lessons if we decide to listen to the words of those who are vulnerable and humble enough to teach us these lessons. Lessons I would ultimately get to understand when I witnessed them for myself.

The Dalai Lama is a man who has experienced great hardship. A man who had no choice but was destined from birth to rule the Tibetan people. He faced war as the leader of his people at the age of sixteen and by his twenties was exiled into India as the Chinese attempted to eradicate the entire Tibetan culture and way of life. The Dalai Lama spoke earnestly about all suffering, "Even a tragic situation can become an opportunity... the suffering is what makes you appreciate the joy." In *The Book of Joy*, by Douglas Abrams, the Dalai Lama shares a story about his friend Lopon-la who was tortured and starved in a labor camp for eighteen years in Siberia. He says his greatest danger was not death or being tortured, but his danger of losing the compassion for his Chinese guards. To listen to people like Archbishop Desmond Tutu talk about his struggles during the apartheid, or contemplate the life of Nelson Mandela after twenty-seven years of imprisonment, and how they both came out on the other side of struggle is astonishing. I think Tutu puts it elegantly, "Our almost natural response is when I'm hit, I hit back. When you have been refined, you want to find out what it is that impelled this other one to do what he did. And so you put yourself in the shoes of the other."

Anne Frank wrote in her diary at the age of thirteen during the holocaust, "In spite of everything, I still believe people are really good at heart." In a similar vein, Viktor Frankl writes in his book, Man's Search for Meaning, on the loss of joy and compassion in concentration camps. But amongst some of the worst atrocities there were individuals that continued to love, continued to have joy and continued to serve one another, including serving the people enslaving them in the first place. Malala Yousafzai, a Pakistani female advocate, survived a bullet shot to the head and she continues to advocate for women's rights to this day.

These stories almost seem surreal. I had struggles in my life, yes, but I've never been tortured in a concentration camp, fled my country, faced relentless prejudice or had fears about where my next meal would come from. No one was trying to kill me for my beliefs. Yet these people have redefined suffering into compassion and grace to show the world that we are all enough. I couldn't see it though because I was lost in the comparison game and therefore believed that in America, I would never touch true suffering; it was always somewhere out there. Then I took a job as a nurse technician at an inpatient oncology floor at my local hospital.

I cannot tell you how many patients I sat with facing the end of their life. The amount of care and compassion I saw on that floor always bewildered me. It did not matter what your story was, your religion, your age, what you did for a living, if you were male or female, black, white or brown, rich or poor, you were equal on this floor. There were no judgments or finger pointing or chest poundings; if you made it to our floor chances were significant that it was the end of the road for you. The end of the road that equalizes us all in the fragility of life. Everyone was suffering, yet everyone also had this posture of vulnerability and humility. They changed my outlook on pain and my notion of first world problems, and they also changed my outlook on being satisfied with "enough." I remember taking care of a woman whose only goal that day was to get chicken noodle soup and the floor was out. She said she'd give a million dollars for some if she had it. I went floor to floor until I found a can of chicken noodle soup. When I returned, her eyes were bigger than a kid discovering ice cream for the first time. Ironically, she was watching the local news announce the lottery winner. She turned to me to say, "I'd share that ticket with you right now if I had it."

I'm human, I still have an ego, and I thought I was a man of strong faith and beliefs and confidence in what I defined as “enough.” Yet this job tested me every time I stepped onto the floor and with every patient I interacted with. I admitted Sam after breast cancer had metastasized and spread throughout her body. At only 42 years old she had weeks to live but refused to go on hospice because her daughter had just given birth to her first granddaughter. Sam’s cancer consumed the right side of her body, her right wrist was so swollen it had the circumference of a football. No morphine or oxytocin could touch the pain she was in day and night as she could not sleep or move but simply sit there cradling her arm.

One night after I took her vitals she asked if I would be willing to go to the cafeteria for her. She missed ordering dinner that night as well as the previous night and room service was now done for the day. When I returned with some chicken and rice she asked me if I could help her get into position to pray. This took me aback. A woman who is dying a slow painful death well before her time, in one of the worst ways possible, next to her daughter and her new granddaughter, knowing her story and the struggles she went through as a single black mother, and now she wants to say grace? Before I could stop myself I mumbled, “Why”? She gazed into my eyes without hesitation and said, “Last night we did not have enough and tonight we have more than enough. Praise be to God.” In an instant I felt like an immature sapling waiting to be destroyed by the next gust of wind as I stood next to a woman whose foundation for joy and gratitude was that of a 300-year-old oak tree.

Sam never stopped thanking me, sharing her gratitude for all I was doing for her. Yet she completely changed my view of suffering, how I defined “enough” and what it meant to be truly vulnerable. She died before I ever took the time to thank her earnestly for how she helped alter my outlook on life. I would like to think that I contributed something to that floor, but I know it will never amount to the way those lives affected me. How those lives taught me when enough really is enough. How those lives taught me to have the strength of vulnerability and humility, even when I'm suffering.

We are all afraid of being vulnerable. Vulnerability can feel like exposing our inner soul to the world to allow others to do with it as they please. But what I've learned the most with vulnerability is while fear may keep us from ever touching it and society may paint you as weak for showing it, vulnerability takes immense strength and courage. Vulnerability is a direct tie into humility and a testament to when enough really is enough. It is no longer about what everyone else thinks or wants, it's about what is already inside of you. We choose to engage the world through our own lenses; it is one of the few things in our control. But more often than not, the lenses we put on in the morning give us a blurry distortion that tell us we are not enough. We are not enough without the bigger house, the better salary, the perfect marriage and kids, or the blissful care-free life. We twist this to then say, "If we are suffering it is because we deserve it."

Your worthiness is not dependent upon the external circumstances in your life or how much suffering you face. Bad things happen to good people without justification. I cannot tell you why kids get cancer or senseless accidents happen, why natural disasters happen or human disasters happen. I cannot give justifications for why there is so much pain and brokenness in this world. But I can tell you that we are in control of how we respond to it and how we respond to our suffering. Suffering does not determine our worthiness but our gratitude can set us free from the control suffering has on our life. If you don't believe me, volunteer with a hospice organization or spend time with elders in your nursing home communities. Ask their opinions, you might be surprised at what you hear.

Again, it's not about being grateful <u>for</u> all things, it's about having the ability to be grateful <u>in</u> all things. I promise you that the more you walk through this desert, the more you open up to the possibility of vulnerability and letting go of the fears, the more gratitude you will find, and the more you will realize that you are in fact already enough — just the way you are.

CHAPTER 12 NOTES AND REFLECTIONS

In what ways do you believe you are not enough? In what ways do you project onto others that they are not enough? Do your roots of joy and gratitude feel more like a sapling or an old oak tree?

13

FINDING CONNECTIONS:

letting go of the toxic and finding the new

We are all on the exact same journey together as we are born on this Earth and our life will end here. There is no denying that, but it does not mean we are all on the same path or on the same timeline. Sometimes doing the hard work of entering your desert means making new connections with people that can understand and engage you where you are at on your journey; people who have either been there and can help guide you, or people who are just going to support you without bias.

It was Christmas 2016 and my family was taking a gag test based on your level of empathy called The Empathy Quotient. I thought I did not do well on the test until every family member and friend who had taken it scored significantly lower. It became a competition to see who would end up scoring the lowest. It made my stomach tie into knots. How could this possibly be exciting? It felt like taking a test on how much you could harm and negate someone else's emotions. Then it dawned on me; empathy is not something you are born with, it is something you must learn. You cannot have empathy towards another human if you cannot respect another human and you cannot have respect and empathy towards another human until you are willing to have respect and empathy towards yourself. It is no longer about saying you are right, it's about saying you have made mistakes and you could be wrong. That's one of the places you can engage yourself from. This then allows you to sit with another and hear their pain without trying to judge it, correct it or tell them what they did wrong. Instead you can simply listen and say, "I'm with you in this." Had I not been graced by all of those wonderful souls sharing stories of such brokenness, I wondered if I too would be cheering for a low score.

Vulnerability is not just about engaging ourselves and our story, it has a direct tie into our ability to engage with others. Empathy isn't just about listening to someone. To be empathetic means we can see that person for all that they are going through, which often involves feeling our own pain. Our ability to engage empathy with others means we have to be vulnerable with that person's struggle. While this may sound like it has a negative connotation, this too is actually about finding more joy through the connections with those around us. Joy comes to us more often through despair than through buying that shiny new car. That is why engaging vulnerability to find empathy can be so important.

Let's start off simple with everyday struggles in our relationships. When we go to argue with someone over any matter — politics, religion, societal issues, mistakes, stories, opinions or facts, we often engage from a place of, "I know it all and I have it figured out ... I just need to jam this down your throat until you agree with my point of view." How often does that really work? The answer is it doesn't. Even if that person backs down and says you're right, it's usually because they see no point in even talking with you because it's not a conversation, it's a battle. Battles are only won when someone else loses. I grew up in a family where you did not have to be right, you only had to prove the other person was wrong — that was how you won an argument.

The problem when you are not willing to admit that you may be wrong is there is no conversation to be had. There is no actual communication and the result is no one will listen to you and you will not listen to anyone else. We take on God complexes of ourselves as all-knowing creatures who have it all figured out. The result? People dislike us, they avoid talking to us, and they tend to think even less about whatever idea or cause it was that we were fighting so diligently for in the first place. We become so afraid of being wrong that we convince ourselves there is no other option. When fear controls the argument at the end of the day, whether it is the fear of being wrong or the fear of trying to control outcomes and expectations, it will still ultimately consume us and us alone. This leads us further down the path of disconnection, not unity. It takes us further and further away from our ability to be vulnerable and have empathy with another. If we can't trust each other with the surface level issues in life, how are we going to trust each other in our pain and despair?

What if when I lost "everything" I actually lost nothing at all? I have come to learn that connection is synonymous with joy and love. In the reverse, disconnection is synonymous with pain and despair. Money, success and save the world projects brought me further into disconnection with not only my new family, but my friends and the people I was trying to serve. The more successful I was, the more I became encapsulated in pain and despair. It wasn't until I lost everything that I was able to begin to find connections and joy in my life again. It wasn't until I lost everything that I actually had the time to serve others and take a break from serving myself. Only when I stopped trying to serve myself was I able to be present with vulnerability and empathy for those around me.

If you choose to enter the desert, it's important to surround yourself with people that love you and support you for who you are. Anyone trying to change you or tell you what you should or should not be doing is toxic, especially during a time of transformation when you are most vulnerable. We all think we have figured it out and know what is best; trust me, I've been in those shoes. When someone knows "what is best" though, it is their baggage they are trying to project onto you and in times of walking through the desert, it is not your job to help anyone else handle their baggage. I say this bluntly because usually what is best is not more advice or more judgment, but unconditional love and support. This is what creates a safe space for us to further engage our own issues and find the courage to face them so they are no longer controlling us. If the world could be fixed through advice, don't you think it would have worked by now? This is not to say advice cannot be helpful. When you are ready for it and when you are open to hearing it, it's great to ask for it and to seek that wisdom from others. But if you are not asking for it, then unsolicited advice is like rubbing salt in the wound. The people you need to connect with are the people that are going to watch you struggle and not try to fix it, not try to tell you what you're doing wrong, but sit with you in your pain and stay there regardless; people who have the strength to engage in vulnerability and empathy themselves.

Remember, this is about you and your journey and only you can inevitably take it, no one else can do that for you. So when it comes to making new connections, there is already enough negativity in the world — on TV, in the news or on social media. We do not need any more of it in our lives. This is our opportunity to seek positive support to encourage us on our path in the desert, not attempt to derail us. Don't be surprised if it can't be found in your existing friends or family; in my experience that can be some of the worst places to find it as we can have a long history and biases with those around us. I can assure you that there are people walking or who have walked through pain and despair everywhere. Whether that is a mentor, a therapist or a support group, these are the people that have found strength in vulnerability to do the hard work. The minute you begin to share your vulnerability and struggles, a whole new world will begin to open. A world where you will find yourself in control of saying yes and no to things based on what is best for you, not because fear is pushing you to.

Before you engage in anything to say yes or no, take time to understand why you are answering that way. Brian McLaren's book on *Naked Spirituality* is a great reference for this. He talks about how saying "yes" can lead to a life of abundance, but it can also come with a lot of false connections. Sometimes we say "yes" because we think it will get us something or somewhere, we might say "yes" because we want to appear to other people in a certain way, or because that person may be important on some level or it is a disguise to please our self. The opposite can also be equally dangerous when a "no" is not really a no. This happens when we say "no" to something because we don't want to face it, or be exposed, perhaps to teach another person a lesson or because we are not "those" things ("those" implying another way to protect our image).

When we decide whether to say yes or no to something, we have a chance to step into our authenticity. Authenticity means letting go of the shoulds and oughts that come with fear, and engaging who we really are at the soul level. This cannot exist if we do not have a firm grasp on our sense of vulnerability and empathy because no genuine decisions can be made without it. What is it that makes you thrive? Being authentic to our true self frees us from all the constraints we place upon ourselves. If you can't take yourself seriously by saying yes to yourself, then you cannot expect anyone else to. It is why empathy and compassion start with having it on yourself. Then, the more time we sit with our authentic self, finding wholeness within, the more chances we have to gain new wisdom and insights into who we really are and what is really best for us.

In this process of finding new connections with our self and those around us, we will gain new wisdom and insights that take us a step forward in the world. Fear begins to lose its hold on us and we start seeing with new eyes. Perhaps we have more patience with ourselves, care more about others or hold less prejudice on issues. This process of making new connections does not have to be earth shattering or involve deep heartfelt conversations with every person you meet. It can be as simple as giving yourself the day off, writing a letter to a grandparent, smiling at a stranger, or baking cookies to let your mail person or janitor know you care and are thankful for what they do to make your life a little bit easier. Sometimes vulnerability and empathy are best shown through acknowledging that you and those around you are seen and that we all matter.

In order to start finding new connections again, even if it's new connections with old friends and family, you have to continue to engage vulnerability and empathy over and over again to let go of that desire to be right or that desire to try and control outcomes. Sticking to your guns does not foster healthy relationships, compassion and grace does. Everything we discuss in this book is like a muscle — the more you practice it, the stronger it gets. But you cannot expect to go from never exercising one day, to running a marathon the next. You have to practice, a lot, and it takes time. Have grace on yourself for all of the mistakes you are going to make on this journey because it will then allow you to have more grace on those you engage with. This only makes your connections stronger and finding new connections will come easily as you begin to surround yourself with people who have more compassion, vulnerability and empathy. To put it very plainly, hate only breeds more hate, but love, love has the possibility to transform fear into something far greater.

CHAPTER 13 NOTES AND REFLECTIONS

What connections in your life do you need to lose that are toxic to your well being? Do you have the strength to sit unbiasedly with others? Do you need to find new connections so that someone can sit unbiasedly with you?

14

FINDING GRACE:

like everything else, it still starts with you

The more we find ourselves filled with grace, the easier the walk in the desert becomes, the easier our relationships become and the easier life in general becomes. Grace allows us to mold fear into a force for good but it starts with you. If you cannot give yourself grace well, then you cannot receive grace well, and if you cannot receive grace well, then you cannot give grace to another well. Grace begins with knowing you are imperfect and make lots of mistakes, will continue to make mistakes, yet you will love yourself anyway. Guilt and shame cannot ultimately create change because you will not be coming from that place of authenticity. Ask anyone with any addiction they have ever struggled with how many times they have fallen back into the same old patterns over and over again. Typically, we try and break our patterns because we feel like we should or we feel guilt over the actions in the first place. We then wonder why we constantly fail when we try to change these behaviors because we inevitably want to keep doing that thing in the first place. It takes a change in mindset to break any addiction, it takes understanding what is the driving motivator in the first place. It typically isn't just one answer, it typically isn't black and white, and you cannot take that journey in the desert if you are not willing to have compassion to forgive yourself for where you came from.

I will never forget the first time my daughter ran away. She was taking a nap in the house and I was sitting in the back yard working. I had the windows open with a ten-foot gap between us so I could hear her if she woke up early. About thirty minutes later I heard someone pounding on my neighbor's door. I thought it was a salesman and I was hoping they would not try and bang on my door and wake my daughter up. They must have been knocking on this house for five minutes and I thought nothing of it. Then my phone rang; a friend of mine who was a police officer that quite frankly never calls. He informed me one of his co-workers had my daughter out front. I damn near fainted. I walked the fifty feet to the front of my house to see the neighbors quickly disperse to avoid making eye contact with me. My two-and-a-half-year-old daughter stood there wearing goggle sunglasses, in her underwear, completely covered from head to toe in marker. I quickly realized she never took a nap, walked right out the door, went across the street and for thirty minutes the neighbors had been trying to find the parents to this lost child. I had no excuse. I was not listening to music, I did not leave the house, I was literally feet away the entire time ignoring neighbors who turned out to be searching for me. The only thing that ran through my head over and over again was "father of the year."

This is how kids get abducted, hit by cars, end up drowning in swimming pools, and I began challenging every notion of my ability to parent a child. I was ashamed, I was embarrassed and I felt unworthy to call myself a dad. Her mother called and I braced for the worst, yet all she could do was pour grace on to me and tell me to stop being so hard on myself. Out of nowhere friends and strangers flooded me with their "parent of the year" stories. Kids caught eating feces, accidents that caused their kid to break a bone, kids escaping the house at three in the morning, leaving kids at the mall, racing kids to the ER, and little by little I began to breathe.

This was not the first time I was going to make a mistake this significant, but if I let it dictate how I defined myself, I would ultimately fail my child and myself. Grace starts with yourself because when you forgive yourself you are able to take a step forward. When you are able to take that step forward you will now accept grace from other people who share their stories and struggles and mistakes with you, to let you know you are not alone. And when you can start allowing other people to share their grace and compassion with you, you can then be the friend or stranger on the street that has grace and compassion on someone else when they make a mistake or their kid runs away. Authenticity does not come from telling someone what they should or should not be doing, authenticity comes from a place of saying that I've been there, I've done that, I know your pain, I see your fears, I understand your shame and I'm willing to love you anyway because we are all in this together.

When shame and guilt, shoulds and oughts, judgments and resentments are no longer in control of you, that is when you know that fear is no longer in control. Fear is no longer in control because you are beginning to release your own control over the outcomes and expectations in life. You are beginning to realize that you and those around you are enough, regardless of imperfections or differences. This is when you start taking steps to come out of the desert, this is where you begin to see with new eyes, this is where you being to live again.

CHAPTER 14 NOTES AND REFLECTIONS

How might you have grace and compassion on yourself? Do you let others have compassion on you? How might you show grace and compassion to others? What mistakes have you made that you need to give yourself grace for?

15

ENDING THE CYCLE:

your new life starts here

Part of ending our cycle with fear is taking that next step forward to help serve others. Once we become stable in ourselves and with who we are, it becomes easier to help those around us. Sometimes it is easy to associate needs with finances. A homeless person needs a place to sleep, sure. But we all have needs. We all need to feel a part of something bigger than ourselves. That includes the need to feel heard and the need to feel loved, but don't be afraid to take vulnerability to the next level and make it practical. The more practical it becomes, the easier and safer it becomes for everyone involved. Needing help is often seen as a weakness, but I would argue that trying to not need help is an insecurity of being perceived as weak – overcoming insecurities and asking for help is a sign of true strength. Instead of rushing around killing yourself to try and prove you have it all together, ask for help. Start simple if you have to. Could you watch my kid, could I borrow a tool, could you give me directions, could you advise me how to make this meal, how to fix this leak or how to read this report? Great leaders and business people do not have it all figured out. They are humble enough to know that it takes a team to pull something off because no one can be every one. We may have to enter our desert alone, but when we step back out, we cannot truly thrive in life alone. We flourish based on our interconnectedness, not our ability to live independently.

Try and engage your conversations in a two-fold manner. Start by pondering a straightforward question; what if your eyes could help me see something that I could otherwise not see? Then we can engage the second part when we realize that we all have something to offer (big or small) and we all have worth in this world. When you share your gifts in the world, it's amazing what you can receive in return.

I was out for a walk with my daughter when she was barely a year old. I came upon an older lady carrying a box that she was resting up against a retaining wall of someone's yard. I asked her if she needed help carrying that box home. She did not speak English, but she didn't need words to express the relief that overcame her when I took it off her hands. We were two blocks away from Goodwill and to be honest, I was shocked she made it that far. There must have been thirty pounds of ceramic cups and plates in that box and as it turned out, she didn't live around the corner but almost a mile away. It took me twenty-five minutes to carry a box that would have taken her hours. I'd had years of studying Spanish, so we managed to mumble together incomplete sentences back and forth. We had enough to understand each other and share stories and matters of the heart. By the time I arrived at her home, her mother, who must have been in her nineties, greeted me with a big hug begging me to come inside for tacos. Financially they had so little, but spiritually they had so much to give to me. I didn't do anything big or noteworthy or sexy in the eyes of the public but the love and grace I received from across a cultural barrier with hardly the means to communicate sticks with me to this day. All because I had a simple gift to offer her and she had many gifts to offer me.

There is a beautiful phrase in the Bible called Imago Dei meaning we are all "made in the image of God," or made in the gift of divine love. Whether you are spiritual or not, somewhere along the way you have received love as a gift. It is meant to be shared especially if we want to keep receiving it. I would like to suggest that with every person we encounter, we have the opportunity to have grace, compassion and love towards them. We hardly ever know the extent of the other person's story but that also means we don't always know the extent of the affect our love, grace and compassion will have on them. When we get lost in questions like "why bother?" they become forms of keeping the cycle going. It is a question that protects our fears. "Why bother" keeps us safe from opening up to somebody who could hurt us but also to somebody who may need us, somebody who could love us and ultimately to someone who may have gifts they could share back with us. Gifts that we may not even know we need. One of the greatest gifts we have in this life is the opportunity to love every person we encounter. Even if that is a complete stranger we may never see again or that person we disagree with so much we can't stand to be around them. I think Mother Theresa put it best, "Each time anyone comes into contact with us, they must become better people from having met us, we must radiate God's love." We all have the opportunity to radiate love.

My hope for you is that you find yourself lucky enough to engage your despair, with enough strength to walk into that desert, enough support to encourage you to keep walking when everything tells you to turn away, and enough grace and compassion to see yourself walk back out the other side. It took me four walks in the desert over the course of a year, after four years of struggling to enter the desert in the first place, before I could start writing this book. Whether it takes you one try or a hundred tries, I hope the day comes when you are no longer a sapling getting tossed about by the slightest breeze, but you find your foundation in joy with roots as strong as an oak tree. Never forget it's not about being free from fear, it's about becoming comfortable with facing fear and releasing the control it has over us. Only when we can sit with and face our fears are we no longer running from them.

Thank you for taking the time to let me share part of my story with you and thank you for all of the wonderful gifts that you bring into this world, even the ones you don't know that you have.

Resources

For future events, books or to request speaking engagements as well as any questions, comments or concerns, please contact us at: **info@ThadCummings.com**
www.ThadCummings.com

The Book of Joy: Lasting Happiness in a Changing World
by Dalai Lama, Desmond Tutu, and Douglas Carlton Abrams

The Gifts of Imperfection: Let Go of Who You Think You're Supposed to Be and Embrace Who You Are
by Brené Brown

How to Be Here: A Guide to Creating a Life Worth Living
by Rob Bell

The Four Agreements: A Practical Guide to Personal Freedom
by Don Miguel Ruiz and Janet Mills

Naked Spirituality: A Life with God in 12 Simple Words
by Brian D. McLaren

Anne Frank: The Diary of a Young Girl
by Anne Frank and B.M. Mooyaart

Man's Search for Meaning
by Viktor E. Frankl and William J. Winslade

Wilderness Within Retreat
Kent Dobson, www.kentdobson.com

Free Wheelchair Mission
Don Schoendorfer, www.freewheelchairmission.org